Berlitz ®

Costa Blanca

D1639222

- A ☛ in the text denotes a highly recommended sight
- A complete A–Z of practical information starts on p.99
- Extensive mapping on cover flaps and throughout text

Costa Blanca

Text by David Henderson
Updated by Josephine Hodgson
Photography: Ken Walsh, David Henderson,
   and Claude Huber
Cover Photography: APA/Gregory Wrona
Layout: Media Content Marketing, Inc.
Cartography by Ortelius Design
Managing Editor: Tony Halliday

Ninth Edition 2004 (Reprinted 2004)

CONTACTING THE EDITORS
Every effort has been made to provide accurate information in this publication, but changes are inevitable. The publisher cannot be responsible for any resulting loss, inconvenience or injury. We would appreciate it if readers would call our attention to any errors or outdated information by contacting Berlitz Publishing, PO Box 7910, London SE1 1WE, England. Fax: (44) 20 7403 0290;
e-mail: berlitz@apaguide.co.uk; www.berlitzpublishing.com

Printed in Singapore by Insight Print Services (Pte) Ltd, 38 Joo Koon Road, Singapore 628990. Tel: (65) 6865-1600. Fax: (65) 6861-6438

Berlitz Trademark Reg. U.S. Patent Office and other countries. Marca Registrada. Used under licence from the Berlitz Investment Corporation

050/409 RP

CONTENTS

THE REGION
AND THE PEOPLE

A thousand years ago, the North Africans thought that the Costa Blanca was a paradise, a fragment from the next world that had fortunately fallen onto this one. They had a point. Ten months a year, a blazing sun warms beaches, ochre plains and misty, wind-sculpted mountains. Olive, eucalyptus and carob trees dot ancient fields. Orange groves fill the valleys, and in January and February the mountains burst into colour with pink-and-white almond blossoms.

Spain's fabulous 'White Coast' was christened 2,500 years ago by Greek traders, who founded the colony of *Akra Leuka* (White Headland), on a site near today's Alicante. The Romans called the provincial capital *Lucentum,* City of Light. The letters 'AL' and 'LA' *(Lucentum Alicante)* are proudly displayed on Alicante's city crest.

But the exceptional tourist potential of the Costa Blanca's sun, sea and mountains remained unexploited until the early 1960s, when *alicantinos* looked north to the Costa Brava and south to the Costa del Sol and suddenly realised that they could offer something just as good, if not better. From that moment, *el boom,* as the local people call it, was inevitable. Benidorm, once populated by fishermen, sprouted scores of hotels and hundreds of apartments and villas to accommodate nearly 200,000 holidaymakers a day in summer. A four-lane superhighway (with minor interruptions) follows the coast from the French frontier as far as Alicante, and every year several million tourists speed along it to the burgeoning resorts.

Merely defining the Costa Blanca calls for a word about contemporary Spanish politics. Since the restoration of democracy and the decentralisation of power, the *comunidades autónomas* (regional governments) have taken over their own touristic destiny. The name 'Costa Blanca', hitherto a generality, now belongs exclusively to the authorities in Valencia. The coast from San Pedro del Pinatar to Aguilas, pertaining to Murcia, is officially known as the *Costa Cálida*. The southern-most strip is now called the *Costa del Almería*. This book touches on all three regions, and even ventures into a corner of the *Costa del Azahar*.

But the visitor is rarely aware of these subtleties on the strangely beautiful coastline, extending from beachy Denia to Cape Gata via the tourist metropolis of Benidorm and the bustling port of Alicante. On the southern stretch of the coast, the Mar Menor offers superb facilities and natural wonders, and beyond historic Cartagena lie the unspoiled beaches of Garrucha, a campers' paradise.

Inland there are winding country roads that climb hillsides first terraced by the Moors, serving picturesque vil-

The coast's idyllic beaches draw holidaymakers by the thousand every year.

Colourful façades in dusty pink, golden yellow and sky-blue brighten the streets of Benidorm.

lages unchanged for centuries. Enter the impressive Moorish fortress of Guadalest through a 1000-year-old tunnel and still the only way in. At Elche, a favourite excursion spot, thousands of palm trees, originally planted by the Carthaginians, form Europe's largest date-palm forest, recently designated a UNESCO World Heritage Site. It is rivalled by only one other, 30km (19 miles) away at Orihuela, a charming town on the banks of the River Segura.

For lovers of the past, there are fine examples of Spanish art and architecture, starting with the exceptional Bronze Age gold artefacts on display in Villena. Examples of Francisco Salzillo's Baroque polychrome wood sculpture are to be found in almost every church in his native province of Murcia, and the processional figures carved by the modern

Valencian sculptor, Mariano Benlliure, bring many visitors to the village of Crevillente at Easter.

Entertainment for everyone is within easy reach on the Costa Blanca including a wide variety of sports such as bowling, water-skiing, windsurfing, kite-surfing, scuba-diving, tennis and golf. You can see top matadors fight in *corridas* in the major towns or, preferable for some, visit a safari park, where giraffes roam free in the Spanish wilds. There are gargantuan barbecues where you can feast on regional cooking with more than 1,000 other guests, plenty of fabulous clubs and the Costa's answer to the Guggenheim: the fascinating (and visually stunning) new City of Arts and Sciences in nearby Valencia.

Spain is celebrated for its fiestas, and one of the most spectacular is Villajoyosa's 'Moors and Christians' extravaganza with its re-enacting of old rivalries. Even more dra-

Despite the tourist boom, in many of the region's villages the pace remains slow, as it has for centuries.

Orange groves fill the valleys of the Costa Blanca, thriving in the Mediterranean climate.

matic is Alicante's famous *Hogueras de San Juan* in June, in which giant effigies are burned at midnight, a legacy from a pagan mid-summer sacrifice to the fire gods.

Although tourism is the major industry now in this area, agriculture thrives on reliable underground water supplies and age-old crafts continue to flourish. Paper, shoes, toys and dolls are profitable exports, and lace, cane and esparto grass-work are important cottage industries. At Jijona, factories continue to make *turrón* – a honey-and-almond sweet – much in the same way as the Moors once did. Torrevieja's ancient salt industry remains one of Europe's largest.

The peoples of Valencia, Alicante, Murcia and Almería speak a bewildering variety of dialects: *valenciano, lemosín, alicantino* and *murciano*. The 'local' languages are growing in importance; even street and road signs use them. But everyone speaks Castilian, Spain's official language, as well. Learn a few words and doors will open to you – it's that kind of place.

A BRIEF HISTORY

Nothing has had a greater impact on the Costa Blanca than foreign invasion: Iberians, Phoenicians, Greeks, Romans, Visigoths and Moors had moulded Spain's Mediterranean shores centuries before international tourism gained a foothold. But before any of these were the Costa Blanca's first inhabitants: known as Neanderthal men, they lived primitively and spent a large part of their time hunting. Then, as the Stone Age came to an end, short dark-skinned Iberians started to make their way from North Africa to the Spanish Peninsula. These fierce fighters skilled in guerrilla warfare roamed the Mediterranean foothills, painting a vivid record of their battles on the walls of their rock shelters.

The Celts began to flood into Spain from the north sometime after 900BC They settled in the north and west of the country, never penetrating as far as the Costa Blanca. In central Spain they were slowly absorbed by the reluctant Iberians, but elsewhere both tribes kept fiercely apart, establishing from the first the renowned independence that still characterises Spain's provinces.

Early Traders

The Phoenicians ventured across the Mediterranean from present-day Lebanon, reaching Spain by about 1100BC. They founded many trading settlements in the 'remote' or 'hidden land' they named *Span* or *Spania*. The Costa Blanca was soon dotted with such Phoenician towns as Elche and Játiva.

After about 650BC, Greek traders arrived on the coast to compete for Spain's rich mineral deposits and fertile land. The influence of Greece was short-lived, although the olive the grape, Greek legacies, are still cultivated in the region.

The caves of Almanzora, once inhabited by Stone Age man, are now home to local gypsies.

The Carthaginians, a people related to the Phoenicians, came from North Africa and subsequently took over much of southern Spain, beginning with Cádiz in 501BC The town had sought help from the Carthaginian army in its war against local tribes, and the 'invited guest' decided to stay. The main centre of Carthaginian power in Spain was located on the Costa Blanca: Carthago Nova, now Cartagena, followed in prominence by Alicante.

Carthage, challenged by Rome in the First Punic War (264–241BC), lost most of her neglected holdings in Spain through Iberian attacks. But Carthage's luck changed with an initial victory in the Second Punic War (218–201BC). Hannibal, the Carthaginian general, led one of history's greatest military marches the length of the Costa Blanca to France and Italy, crossing the Pyrenees and the Alps, in the hope of surprising an unsuspecting Rome. The Romans responded by invading Spain to cut off Hannibal's supply route and staying there 600 years.

Under Roman Rule

It took the Romans almost 300 years to subdue the Iberian tribes. Outpost duty was decidedly unpopular with the legionnaires, but the Roman army finally prevailed.

There's no doubt that the Roman presence in Spain had a great influence on the country, bringing the gifts of engineering and architecture. Stability and unity were promoted by the introduction of Latin, from which modern Spanish developed, and Roman law is still the basis of Spain's legal system.

But the Roman empire, overstretched and increasingly corrupt, began to crumble. The Romans withdrew from Spain, leaving the country to be overrun by various barbarian tribes, especially the appropriately named Vandals. These tribes were eventually subdued by the Visigoths, who controlled much of southern Spain for some 300 years. But they did not integrate, nor did they learn the lessons of history; in a palace intrigue, one faction invited the Moors into the country as their allies.

Moorish Domination

In AD711, the Arab chief Tariq landed at Gibraltar with 12,000 Berber troops. Thus began an 800-year epoch of Christian opposition to the newly arrived Muslims (Moors). Within 10 years their green-crescent standard flew over most of Spain. Kartajanah, Mursiyah and Xativa are still known by their Moorish names.

The Moors were relatively tolerant rulers who taxed nonbelievers rather than trying to convert them. They introduced the manufacture of paper, which is carried on today in Játiva.

They laid out a system of irrigation still in use in the Guadalest Valley and filled the *huertas* (orchards) of the Costa Blanca with oranges, peaches and pomegranates. Rice, cotton and sugar cane were also first cultivated on Spanish soil by the Moors.

Numerous Moorish fortifications on the Costa Blanca survive to this day, and the pottery of the region still reflects the influence of Moorish craftsmen. Learning was considerably advanced by the Moors, and a medical treatise written by an Arab physician in Crevillente is recognised today as revolutionary for its time.

The Tide Turns

But, like the Visigoths, the Moors ignored history. Feeling the rising strength of Christianity and weakened by constant fighting among themselves, they sought outside help from the Almohades. These fanatical Berber warriors from

Young women dress up in traditional finery for the Festival of the Moors and Christians.

eight months in 1813. What the world knows as the Peninsular War (1808–1814) is referred to in Spain as the War of Independence, and the country's first, though short-lived, constitution was drafted during this period.

From Decline to Chaos

Hopes of setting up a constitutional monarchy were quickly dashed, and Spain was plunged into a century of power struggles at home. Overseas, her American colonies revolted and gained independence. Soon there was little left of the once great Spanish empire, and an attempt in 1873 to form a republic failed. In 1902, Alfonso XIII became king at the age of 16. His reign was a difficult time for Spain; prosperi-

A breathtaking view of Alicante from the Castillo de Santa Bárbara.

ty and stability eluded the country, which remained neutral during World War I. In 1923, assailed by economic problems and with catastrophe imminent, the king accepted a general, Miguel Primo de Rivera, as dictator. Six years later the opposition of radical forces resulted in Primo de Rivera's fall. Neither reform nor the maintenance of order seemed possible. In 1931 the king himself went into exile following anti-royalist election results, and another republic was founded.

Parliamentary democracy was impeded by the ideological commitment of various political factions and compromise was rare. Spain floundered in a sea of political strikes and violence. Then the Left won the 1936 elections and was immediately in violent collision with the Right.

In July 1936, a large section of the army under General Francisco Franco rose in revolt against the government. On Franco's side were monarchists, conservatives, the Church and the right-wing Falangists. Against him was a collection of republicans, liberals, socialists, communists and anarchists. The ensuing Civil War became one of the great crusades of the 20th century. Germany and Italy supplied Franco's Nationalists with arms and air power, and the Soviet Union gave aid to Spain's communists.

To many people in Europe, often unaware of, or indifferent to, the particular Spanish origins of the struggle, the Civil War was seen as a crucial conflict between democracy and dictatorship, or, from the other side, as one of law and order against social revolution and chaos. The bloodshed lasted for three years and cost hundreds of thousands of lives.

Even after the war, the hardship continued. But despite pressure from Hitler, Franco, Spain's new *caudillo* (leader), managed to keep his exhausted country out of World War II.

Modern Times

During the years of post-war reconstruction, Franco encouraged tourism on a grand scale as a way to bring currency into the country. Profoundly affecting the economy and the people, this transformed Spain's most attractive coasts, though not always for the better. When the *caudillo* died in 1975, Prince Juan Carlos, the grandson of the Bourbon King Alfonso XIII, succeeded to the Spanish throne. The new king led the way from totalitarianism to democracy. A new constitution granted wide-ranging powers to the regions. In 1986 Spain entered the European Community, ending decades of isolation. While membership brought much-needed funds into the country, troubles such as inflation, unemployment, crime and pollution led to the Conservative Party's defeat of the Socialist Party in the 1996 elections, after 13 years of dominance. In January 2002 Spain became one of the 12 EU countries to adopt the euro.

This architectural innovation steals the scene in Calpe.

WHERE TO GO

With such a long stretch of coast to cover and so many historic towns to visit inland, the Costa Blanca may seem difficult to navigate – particularly if you don't have a car. But the itineraries in the following pages take in all the tourist-worthy sights in this sprawling region, and every one of these important places of interest can easily be reached by public transport.

Most visitors will be staying within easy reach of Alicante, so our trips start out from here. At the centre of the region's road network, Alicante is also a logical base for motorists and for train and bus connections. Tourists who fly into Alicante's airport on package holidays usually begin their sightseeing with a visit to the provincial capital.

From Alicante we head north along the coast to Gandia and south to Cartagena. We then make for the historic inland towns of Elche, Orihuela and Murcia, equally within easy reach.

The Essentials

There are certain sights no visitor to the Costa Blanca should miss. If time presses and you have to make a choice, bear in mind these highlights:

Alicante	Castillo de Santa Bárbara
North Coast	Villajoyosa
Benidorm	Guadalest
South Coast	Cartagena
	Mojácar
Inland	Elche
	Catedral de Orihuela
	Catedral de Santa Maria
	and Museo Salzillo (Murcia)

Benidorm is the main destination for many tourists, and this popular town provides another good point of departure for excursions to nearby islands such as the Isla de Benidorm, as well as to moody villages, including Guadalest, in the interior.

The southernmost stretch of coast south of Cartagena is not readily accessible by bus or train. But motorists as well as adventurers willing to brave infrequent, capricious transport services will enjoy discovering the few remaining pockets of unspoiled arid beauty and remote whitewashed villages. Most of this coast, though, is filling with hotels, villas and apartment blocks.

Signs:
entrada – **entrance**
salida – **exit**
rebajas – **sale**
servicios – **toilets**
completo – **full**
   (eg hotel)

ALICANTE

Swaying palms and luminous skies, along with some of Spain's best restaurants and *tapas* bars, lure visitors to the provincial capital of Alicante. The town is as popular with European holidaymakers today as it was with Greek and Roman colonisers in ancient times.

You'll always see cosmopolitan crowds here, especially on the **Explanada de España**, the splendid waterfront promenade that stretches alongside the harbour, and on the Paseo Maritimo. You can stroll to the music of the municipal band on Sundays or try one of the restaurants on the Paseo. Just east of the Explanada, an irresistible stretch of sandy beach, the Playa del Postiguet, beckons.

The broad **Rambla de Méndez Núñez**, running at a right angle to the Explanada, is good for a morning's shopping and has a lively market at one end. It's also the route taken by patriotic, civic and religious processions, most notably the *Hogueras de San Juan* parade held every June. Off the *rambla* (a broad tree-lined avenue) to the right is the Calle Mayor, a pedestrian street. Here, street vendors hawk pens, watches and jewellery, and on religious holidays processions pass by on their way from the **Catedral de San Nicolás de Bari**. Situated a stone's throw from the Calle Mayor on Avenida General Sanjurjo in the old town, the cathedral was considerably restored after the Civil War. Note the impressive nave and façade, excellent examples of the austere style

Getting Around

By train

The principal routes are: Valencia–Alicante–Cartagena; Alicante–Madrid; Cartagena–Murcia–Albacete–Madrid, and Alicante–Barcelona. For information, contact Estación de Madrid, RENFE, Avenue Salamanca, Alicante; tel: 902 240 202. There is a train to Denia via Benidorm and Calpe from the FGV Estación de la Marina, Playa del Postiguet; tel: (96) 526 2731.

By coach/bus

Spanish coaches are air-conditioned and comfortable. Ask about tours at your hotel or local tourist office. Buses are cheap (but not as comfortable). Routes include Alicante to Benidorm and Cartagena, and to Murcia, Denia and Alcoy.

The main bus station in Alicante is in Calle Portugal 17; tel: (96) 513 0700.

By car

The important routes are: E-15 expressway south; N-340 (Barcelona–Alicante–Murcia–Cádiz); A-7 toll road (Valencia–Alicante–Murcia); N-332 (Valencia–Alicante–Almería); N-330 (Alicante–Albacete); N-301 (Cartagena–Murcia–Madrid); A-7 (Alicante–Valencia–Barcelona).

of Juan de Herrera (1530–97), recalling the magnificent Escorial Palace near Madrid, which he also designed.

Walk beyond the Calle Mayor and the tranquil Plaza de Santa Faz to get to the Plaza del Ayuntamiento, where a coin and stamp market is held on Sundays and public holidays. The square is the site of the **Ayuntamiento** (Town Hall), with a stunning twin-towered Baroque façade designed in the 18th century by Lorenzo Chápuli, a local architect. A highly polished brass stud on the first step of the main staircase registers a height exactly 3m (10ft) above sea level. This is Spain's official altitude-measuring point. The handsome, red-lettered marble plaque on the same staircase is a copy of the city's charter, presented by Ferdinand II of Aragon in 1490.

The Ayuntamiento houses a small picture gallery and a chapel with tiles from Manises, an important Valencian ceramics centre. Look for the painting of the patron saint of Alicante, Saint Nicholas of Bari, over the altar. There are 18th-century royal portraits in the **Salón Azul** (Blue Room) and archives that preserve the document of privileges granted to the city by Alfonso X, the Wise, in the 13th century.

A short distance uphill brings you to the Plaza Santa María and the magnificent Baroque **Iglesia de Santa María**. The church dates from the 14th century and is one of many built during the Christianisation of territory won from the Moors by James I in legendary 13th-century battles; it stands on the site of a former mosque. Works by Braque, Chagall, Dalí, Picasso and many other 20th-century artists hang next door in the **Museo de la Asegurada** (a museum of 20th-century art). Beyond you'll find the tiny **Barrio de Santa Cruz**. This quarter is all that remains of the

A visitor strolls along the splendid Explanada de España promenade in Alicante.

Villa Vieja, or old town. You can still see fascinating glimpses of traditional narrow streets where houses are decorated with potted plants and wrought-iron grilles.

From this *barrio* you'll be able to see the most prominent sight in Alicante, the historic **Castillo de Santa Bárbara**, perched 115m (350ft) above the city on Mount Benacantil. The site has been fortified since prehistoric times and offers beautiful views of Aitana, San Juan, Santa Pola and Benidorm and Tabarca islands in the distance. To get to the castle, drive up the winding road to the summit or use the lift at the far end of Calle Juan Bautista Lafora, opposite the Postiguet beach. Santa Bárbara, built by the Carthaginians in the third century BC, was so well fortified that for nearly 2,000 years nobody conquered it. While you're there, be

A view of Alicante's Castillo de Santa Bárbara from a nearby orchard.

sure to visit the Collección Capa, a permanent display of contemporary Spanish sculpture.

On the opposite side of town in the Barrio San Blas is the smaller **Castillo de San Fernando**, begun during the War of Independence (1808–1814). The castle, set above the trees of the small **Parque Municipal**, provides a favourite spot for viewing Santa Bárbara and the port in the late afternoon.

The **Museo Arqueológico Provincial**, housed in the former Hospital de San Juan de Díos on Plaza Doctor Gómez Ulla, contains an interesting ceramics collection, with some pieces dating back to the Greeks. Take a look at the graceful pottery of the Iberians, adorned with simple painted lines, and the Stone Age finds, including pottery and bone bracelets. There are also fascinating Carthaginian and Greek carvings and Moorish relics. The museum building is magnificent in its own right.

Outskirts of Alicante

Outside town, on the main Valencia highway, the **Monasterio de Santa Verónica** (Saint Veronica's Monastery) attracts about 15,000 pilgrims and a good many hawkers during the annual May celebration of the *Santa Faz* (Holy Face). Armed with canes decorated with bunches of rosemary, the participants proceed on foot to the monastery, where they venerate the Holy Face cloth. According to tradition, the cloth retained the bloodstained image of Jesus' face after Saint Veronica used it to wipe his brow as he went on his way to Calvary.

The sacred relic was first worshipped in the Alicante region during a drought in 1489. As it was being carried across the site of the present-day monastery, the *Santa Faz* is said to have suddenly become too heavy to hold, and believers claim that a tear fell from the right eye of the image. This was interpreted as a sign to construct the building which has housed the cloth ever since. It can be seen at the high altar or in a chapel off the sacristy.

There are two other Holy Face handkerchiefs – one in Jaén and the other in the Vatican. According to Roman Catholic authorities, the original cloth was divided into three.

Alicante's picturesque marina, flanked by the palm-lined Explanada promenade.

The small, flat island of **Tabarca** lies about an hour by boat from Alicante. Boats run daily from Alicante and Santa Pola, from where the sea voyage takes half as long. You won't see any pirates here, as the last of them sailed away from their former stronghold in 1786. But you will find fishermen, many of whom are direct descendants of some 600 Genoese mercenaries King Charles III rescued from captivity on Tunisia's Tabarka Island, hence the name. These people have made Tabarca their home for more than two centuries, in spite of poor fishing and the lack of doctor, priest and schoolmaster. It was tourism that finally saved the declining population from fading away altogether, and provided islanders with a priest and teacher at last. Sun-seeking visitors, mostly Spaniards, flock to the island on Sundays, the most popular day for excursions. Even then, you'll always be able to find peace and quiet on one of the tiny seaweed-draped coves beyond the main sandy bay.

Inland from Alicante

For a change of scenery, drive north of Alicante into the rocky lunar-like landscape of the Cabeço d'Or mountains. This is where you'll find the **Cuevas de Canalobre** (Candelabrum Cave), which is reached by following the N-340 from San Juan de Alicante until the turn-off for **Busot**, where signs mark the way to the cave. Floodlights dramatise the eerie ranks of gigantic stalagmites and stalactites, which crowd chambers up to 115m (350ft) high. The acoustics are so exceptional that summer concerts are held in the caves.

Jijona also lies within easy reach of the provincial capital. This town, just 27km (14 miles) from Alicante on the N-340, is renowned for the manufacture of *turrón*, an exotic sweet of Moorish origin, made from ground almonds, orange-blossom honey, egg white and sugar. Traditionally served by the

Spanish at Christmas time, there are several different varieties to choose from, including soft, hard and flavoured. You can learn all about this popular confection on a tour of El Lobo factory, founded in 1725. There's even a small museum on the premises.

From Jijona, continue along the N-340 to **Alcoy**, 56km (36 miles) from Alicante. Don't be disappointed by this grey industrial town, for it manufactures some of Spain's most popular sweets: they are *peladillas* (Marcona almonds coated with sugar). Sometimes pine kernels are sugar-coated, too, and the delicious result is known as *pinyonets*.

Alcoy is even more famous for its annual Moros y Cristianos Festival: one of the most colourful and exuberant traditional fiestas in the province. If you're here out of season, the costumes, worn year after year, will be on display in the 18th-century Casal de San Jordi.

The **Museo Camilo Visedo** nearby houses a fascinating collection of Iberian clay sculpture taken from a settlement in the Sierra Serreta. To visit the site, just a few kilometres (a couple of miles) from town, take the C-3313 road, but prepare yourself for a hard 30-minute scramble up the Serreta.

From the town of **Ibi** onwards you'll see many castles and forts, some of them visible for miles. They were strategically positioned by ever-vigilant Romans, Moors and Christians.

The castle of **Castall**, just off the Ibi-Villena road, is one of the most dramatically located in Spain. It was built by the counts of Castalla, but left incomplete. Further along the Villena road is the medieval castle of **Biar**, which has been well restored and is surrounded by a double wall. It was declared a national monument and has magnificent sweeping views of the valley from the battlements.

Continue now to the town of **Villena**, the furthest point from Alicante (64km/39 miles away) on this tour. The **castle** here, noted for its double walls and high, eight-turreted tower rarely found south of Madrid, also has national monument status. Villena's castle was originally built by Moors, though considerable additions were made to the building in the 15th century.

The town's priceless Bronze Age gold artefacts, discovered in a clay jar in the riverbed, are exhibited at the **Museo Arqueológico** within the 16th-century Palacio Municipal (opposite the tourist office) and attest to the artistry of Villena's early inhabitants.

Swing south from Villena along the N-330 to **Sax**, site of the Roman town of Saxum. The towers of the original Roman castle, which has been fully restored, are still a lookout point. Back on the N-330 you soon come to **Petrel**'s

A rooftop view of Alcoy, famous for manufacturing **peladillas,** *a popular Spanish sweet.*

Biar's Moorish castle is perched on a hilltop, one of many castles lining the Ibi-Villena route.

Moorish **castle**, reputed to have fabulous treasure buried in its grounds.

Unrestored medieval fortresses are found along the C-3212 road to **Elda**, and beyond, at **Monóvar**. Elda itself is noted for excellent wine and lace-making. The town was the birthplace of the famous writer, José Martínez Ruiz, better known as Azorín. From Elda, follow the signs to **Novelda** to find yet another Moorish castle set high on a hill. This one is the **Castillo de la Mola**, erected on the site of a Roman fort. It has an unusual triangular tower dating from the 13th century. Right next to it you'll see a strange structure reminiscent of Gaudí's still unfinished Templo de la Sagrada Familia in Barcelona.

If, after all this castle-viewing, you still haven't had enough, a few kilometres further on in **Aspe**, you'll find *las ruinas* (the ruins). Local people will direct you to the castle, which they never call by that name. Look out for Roman and Moorish relics, which are still sometimes discovered around here. Then head back to Alicante, situated just 28km (17 miles) away.

THE NORTH COAST

The Costa Blanca's reputation for magnificent beaches and lively resorts comes from the northern stretch of coast. Take the N-332 from Alicante and drive through **Campello** to the fishing port of **Villajoyosa**. This picturesque village, some 30km (18 miles) from the provincial capital, is more

---

Castles in Spain

The Costa Blanca has a good share of Spain's 5,000 officially classified castles. Some of them are well preserved, while others have been restored. For 700 years Moors and Christians fought each other for possession of many of the castles, with both sides winning and losing, conquering and defending, as the tide of battle turned for or against them.

A castle in Spain is often more than meets the eye, for all have a specific purpose, history and name. *Alcazabas* are castle fortresses built by Moors in isolated places. *Castillos guerreros*, on the other hand, were built by Christians on sites specially chosen for their strategic positions. And then there are the castle citadels, the *alcázares*. Some of the Moorish *alcázares* are magnificently preserved, enclosing gardens with fountains. Christians substituted the greenery with functional courtyards in their severe *alcázares*.

Dreaming of your own Spanish castle? The *Asociación de Amigos de los Castillos*, tel: (96) 590 5324 situated in Alicante's romantic Castillo de Santa Bárbara, strives for the preservation of castles. It also arranges for their sale to private owners – for a price.

Benidorm, one of Spain's most famous resorts, lies just 12km (7½ miles) north of Villajoyosa. On the way, you'll pass the Casino Costa Blanca, where the stakes are low and the excitement runs high. For more information on Benidorm, *see page 43*.

Altea, 10km (6 miles) north of Benidorm, was an important Phoenician port. The Moors called it Altaya, meaning 'Health for All', but not before they

Entrada libre –
admission free
prohibido tomar
fotografías – **no**
cameras allowed.

had destroyed the first settlement and rebuilt the town. Altea is one of Spain's most memorable and tranquil towns, and a careful development policy helps to keep it that way. You'll find small bungalows here, rather than hotel blocks, and a delightful seaside market held on Tuesdays.

The 257 steps that climb steeply above the main shopping street, the Avenida Fermín Sanz Orrio, lead to the old village. Here the streets are almost always full of people, who congregate in local bars and restaurants. Altea has a number of art galleries and a stunning arts centre just northwest of the old town, where concerts and exhibitions are held regularly.

On Sundays and fiestas, traditional games of *pelota* are played in the narrow streets near Altea's church square. Players strike the ball with their bare hands against walls, doors and windows – which are protected by grilles.

The best of the local beaches, most of which are pebbly, is south at **Albir**, between Altea and the Sierra Helada.

Calpe's popularity with tourists is ensured by two fine sandy beaches. This former fishing village (12km/7½ miles from Altea) lies at the base of the **Peñón de Ifach**, a volcanic

Altea, once an important Phoenician port, is now one of Spain's most tranquil towns.

rock thrusting out of the sea to a height of more than 335m (1,000ft). You can take a trip around here in a semi-submersible glass-bottomed boat.

You don't have to be a mountaineer to climb the rock, just reasonably fit. On the way up, you can admire the wild flowers and in autumn and winter you may catch sight of Audouin's Gull (a rare species with dark-olive legs and a black-banded red bill). Take a jacket and something to drink.

If you have time, follow the coastal road from Calpe to **Moraira**, where flats and villas fill terraced hillsides high above rocky coves. Otherwise, take the main Alicante–Valencia road, which passes inland through rich agricultural country to **Gata de Gorgos** – a town noted for cane, basketwork and even furniture – and rural Jávea.

Jávea, 27km (16 miles) from Calpe, sprawls between pine-covered Cape Nao to the south and Cape San Antonio to the north. The town is ideal for a quiet family holiday, especially in spring, when Jávea is magical with the scents of lemon and orange blossoms. Citrus fruit became the region's principal cash crop around the turn of the 20th century when grain and the 17th-century windmills of Cape San Antonio were abandoned. Jávea makes a good base for walking, and the tourist office has several pamphlets detailing walks, both in town and the area. Jávea also has an interesting **Museo Arqueológico y Etnográfico** with an important collection of Iberian finds from Sierra de Montgó, and two strongly contrasting churches – an early 16th-century fortified building, and a modern, boat-shaped structure.

Ten km (6 miles) from Jávea is **Denia**, with long sandy beaches, a lofty brooding castle and 830m (2,500ft) of Mount

At a height of more than 335 m (1,000 ft), the volcanic rock of Peñón de Ifach towers over Calpe.

In Denia, a local fisherman repairs his nets – and gets some sun in the process.

Montgó to climb. On a clear day you can see all the way to Ibiza, 100km (62 miles) away. Denia's rocky coastline also makes it ideal for diving and there are several schools that offer courses. Other popular sea sports here include windsurfing and kite-surfing. You can also catch a ferry from here to Mallorca or Ibiza. Just east of Denia, you can visit the **Cueva de Agua Dulce** (Freshwater Cave) with its two lakes. A little further away near **Vergel**, you can try the well-kept **Safari Park** with animals galore, a fine dolphin show, children's amusement park, refreshments and restaurants.

At **Gandía** (32km/19 miles north of Denia on the N-332), you'll be tempted to spend all your time on the town's broad promenades and 13km (8 miles) of splendid beaches. But it would be a pity to miss the quiet majesty of the **Palacio Ducal**

de los Borja, home of Duke Francisco de Borja (1510–1572), fourth Duke of Gandía, who abandoned worldly pleasures to join the Jesuit order after the death of his wife. The palace, now a Jesuit college, is open to visitors. Guided tours take place hourly in season and visit apartments with superbly tiled floors and the duke's private chapel.

Inland from Gandía

From Gandía, the C-320, then the C-322, lead inland through orange groves, vineyards and slowly rising country to **Játiva**. This 'city of a thousand fountains', huge plane trees and a sprawling fortress, was probably founded by Hannibal in 219BC. Europe's first paper was made here in the 11th century. Both the painter José de Ribera and two infamous popes, Calixtus III and Alexander VI, were born in Játiva. The popes were members of the Borja family, better known to history as Italy's notorious Borgias.

A common sight in Játiva, also known as the 'city of a thousand fountains'.

Seek out Játiva's late-Renaissance **Colegiata** (Collegiate Church) in the Plaza de Calixto III. Just opposite is the **hospital**, ages old but still in use. It's noted for a splendid façade designed in the ornate 15th-century Plateresque style. Find time, too, for the well-presented **Museo Municipal** in Carrer de la Corretgeria 46. In the courtyard round the corner, the 11th-century **Pila de los Moros** (Moorish Basin) was once used for traditional ablutions. The figures decorating the basin are rarely seen in Muslim art, since Islam forbids human and animal representation.

Directly above the old town, the **Ermita de San Feliú** (Saint Felix's Hermitage) commands a wide view. Although it has been a Christian bastion since the third century, it was a pagan sacrificial site long before that. Continue uphill to

Densely packed with charming old houses, Bocairente is a picture-perfect Spanish village.

the fortress, which is, in fact, two castles. Ramparts connect the smaller pre-Roman **Castillo Menor** (Small Castle) with the Roman and post-Roman **Castillo Mayor** (Main Castle), once notorious for its dungeon. Disgraced princes and other noblemen were confined here, their only solace being the ruined 15th-century chapel adjacent.

Leave Játiva on the C-340 and drive up into the highlands where thick-fleeced sheep and isolated farmhouses complete a memorable vista. Pass through **Albaida**, known for its candle-making, and **Onteniente**, an industrial town, to picturesque **Bocairente**. Visit the village during late summer for the festival of folk dancing, or for February's Fiesta of Moors and Christians. The sombre bull-ring was hacked from solid rock for the *Corrida*.

For a town of barely 5,000 inhabitants, Bocairente's two small museums are impressive: the **Museo Histórico** (Historical Museum) is noted for a collection of Stone Age pottery, and the **Museo Parroquial** (Parish Museum) exhibits important paintings by Juan de Juanes, Ribalta and Sorolla. In the hills northeast of town are the **Covetes de Moros** (Moorish Caves). Some were later lived in by hardy Christian holy men. You can walk to them from the town – follow the signs.

BENIDORM

With twin, crescent-moon beaches, 7km (4 miles) of golden sands and an outstanding climate, **Benidorm** is one of Spain's most popular resorts. But it wasn't always so. Despite efforts over 100 years ago by a local entrepreneur, who hoped to bring holiday-makers to the area by a regular stage coach service, large-scale tourism didn't come to Benidorm until the early 1960s. Since then, a mass of apartment blocks and hotels has sprung up and the town has become known as an international fun city. Some five million people pack into the place throughout the year.

Love it or hate it, Benidorm is thoroughly cosmopolitan; restaurants here serve bacon and eggs, *sauerkraut*, *smorgasbord*, and 'tea like mother makes it'. There are bars, cocktail lounges, ritzy restaurants, modern hotels and a vast choice of discotheques and nightclubs. This makes for a happy, human unending noise that contradicts those who say the town's name derives from the *valenciano* words for 'sleep well'.

The delightful **old village**, the size of a postage stamp, is tucked away on the long spur of land that divides the two beaches. A fort stood here until 1812, when British and Spanish troops blew it up while dislodging the French during Spain's War of Independence, leaving only ruins. The great-

At a Benidorm market, the wide variety of appetising fruits attracts a crowd.

Chequerboard tiled floors add a distinctly Spanish touch of glamour to Playa Punta Canfali in Benidorm.

est concentration of shops and entertainments is to be found around the original village. Away from the beaches there's no end to the amusements, from bowling alleys to water slides.

The **Isla de Benidorm**, a wedge-shaped rock of an island you can see from any of Benidorm's beaches, is an unofficial bird sanctuary, uninhabited except for a summer bar. It's a good spot for a picnic and swim, although the water is deep. Glass-bottomed boat trips from Benidorm average 20 minutes each way; make arrangements to return on one of your boatman's later runs.

Inland from Benidorm

The mountains you see off in the distance on Benidorm's horizon are fragrant with wild herbs and lavender, and in July and August the hedges are lush with blackberries that few local people bother to pick. Drive south on the motorway to Villajoyosa, then take the road that leads to **Sella**. The countryside is undistinguished, until suddenly you look down on the emerald-green waters of the **Amadorio Dam**, a favourite haunt of fishermen and discerning picnickers. Within another 5km (3 miles) you arrive at Sella village, dwarfed beneath an extraordinary plateau.

From Sella the road winds higher through terraced hillsides filled with vines until it reaches its highest point at **Puerto de Tudóns** (1,015m/3,345ft). About 8km (5 miles) on, a secondary road leads to **Peñaguila**, an exquisite old Moorish village with a sturdy ruined castle.

At **Benasau**, the Sella road meets the C-3313. To the west (16km/10 miles) lies Alcoy *(see page 30)*, to the east **Confrides**, a picturesque mountain town.

Now make for **Guadalest** (some 10km/6 miles to the east), the Costa Blanca's famed 'eagle's nest' fortress, built by the Moors 1,200 years ago. Inaccessible except for a tunnel carved through 15m (50ft) of solid rock, Guadalest was never conquered, though James I of Aragon took it by siege during the 13th-century Reconquest. The fortress even withstood an earthquake in 1644, as well as attempts by the Austrian Archduke Charles to blast his way in during the War of the Spanish Succession. Despite the coach tours, Guadalest is very pretty and still relatively 'unheritaged'. Wandering round the compact castle, you'll understand why, for lack of space, the belfry had to be built outside, and why the picturesque old cemetery is so small.

From Guadalest, the road leads to the small town of **Callosa de Ensarriá**, centre of the honey industry, where you can taste before you buy, often six or eight different flavours. From Callosa take the Parcent road, follow it for 2.5 km (1½ miles) and make a right-hand turn at the entrance to the **El Algar waterfalls**, a tumbling oasis beneath the massive Sierra Bernia formed by a tributary of the River Guadalest. Leave your car in the parking area and walk to the 27-m (80-ft) falls.

You can swim beneath the falls in chilly waters, then picnic by the cool leafy pools above. It's easy to get away from crowds in this pleasant spot, but if you're in the mood for company, you'll find lots of people in the restaurants near the car park.

The next stop is **Tárbena** (10km/6 miles further along the C-3318), an invigorating mountain village famed for its delicious sausages. They're made from a secret recipe handed down to the present-day villagers by their Mallorcan ancestors, who came here in the early 17th century as part of an official repopulation scheme.

Guadalest, the Costa Blanca's renowned 'eagle's nest' fortress, has a spectacular view.

After Tárbena comes the finest scenery of all: bold, terraced mountains, wide undulating valleys and scattered farms connected by mule tracks. In spring the countryside is covered with the pink and white of almond blossoms, but the road is for all seasons, with groves of gnarled olive trees alongside it, their leaves blowing silver in the evening light. Follow the road to **Coll de Rates**, 500m (1,500ft) above the wide orange-grove and vine-filled plains that sweep up to Jávea, Denia, Gandía and the deep-blue Mediterranean. Further on, take the road to **Jalon**, where in late summer farmers sell muscat grapes to passers-by, and you can buy some of the strong local wine. Or carry on past Orba to Benidoleig and visit the prehistoric caves, **Las Calaveras**. Here high-domed ceilings drip with stalagtites, and human bones more than 50,000 years old have been found.

Six km (3½ miles) more bring you to the highway from where it's less than an hour's drive north to Valencia and the fabulous Ciudad de las Artes y las Ciencias with its planetarium, IMAX cinema and laser show, interactive science museum, aquarium and open-air auditorium.

THE SOUTH COAST

The fishing port and resort of **Santa Pola** (18km, south of Alicante on the N-332) has an extraordinary number of restaurants. Nearby waters, particularly rich in prawns and red mullet, provide all manner of eating houses, both on the beach and in the town, with some of the best seafood on the coast. There's also a 14th-century castle and several good beaches with fine white sand. Thousands of pines, palms, and eucalyptus trees, planted to control shifting sand

The El Algar waterfalls, a tumbling oasis beneath the massive Sierra Bernia.

49

A stately building in bustling Cartagena, once home to Romans, Visigoths and Moors.

lectively as La Manga. The shallow lagoon is calmer and saltier than the Mediterranean, so you sink less easily. It can also be several degrees warmer, which accounts for the thermal breezes and mellow summer temperatures. It's even mildly rich – and becoming richer – in mineral salts.

The Mar Menor is a sportsman's paradise. You can sign up for sailing, scuba-diving and windsurfing courses, and water-ski on its tranquil waters. On shore there is considerable scope for tennis, or you can try clay-pigeon shooting. For golfers there are twin 18-hole Kentucky blue-grass courses, and the local golf club has a ranch that hires out mounts for riding.

The area of Mar Menor is also noted for its windmills, some of them restored to perfect working condition.

La Manga has been developed as a glamorous resort, with a championship calibre golf course, five-star hotels, tennis clubs, restaurants, luxury villas and apartments straddling the 23km (14 miles) of sand that separate the two seas. The mainland side of the lagoon boasts the smaller but thriving resorts of **Santiago de la Ribera** and **Los Alcázares**.

The compact, bustling city of **Cartagena** (26km/16 miles south of Los Alcázares on the N-332) was a major naval port long before Saint James is said to have landed here with the Gospel in AD36. Romans, Visigoths and Moors all squabbled over the strategically positioned town, which was sacked by Sir Francis Drake in 1588 and taken by Archduke Charles in 1707.

Head for the port and the large waterfront **Plaza del Ayuntamiento**. The big, grey, cigar-shaped object you'll see on view here is a submarine, built by the local inventor Isaac Peral and launched in 1888, 10 years too late to make a world record.

Just north of the Plaza, take a coffee at one of the open-air cafés on the traffic-free Calle Mayor. Then head uphill to the **Castillo de la Concepción** at the highest point of the city. The castle dates back to Roman and perhaps even Carthaginian times. It's surrounded by the **Parque de las Torres**, a beautifully landscaped vantage point. The pepper-pot lighthouse in the park, of Roman or Moorish origin, wrecked many a marauding ship when it was blacked out by Cartagena's defenders.

One glance over the almost landlocked harbour explains why Andrea Doria, the 16th-century Genoese admiral, remarked that the Mediterranean had only three safe ports: June, July and Cartagena. You'll also see why Cartagena is

Windsurf on the open sea, or on the Mar Menor, a salt-water lagoon stretching along the south coast.

called the 'City of Castles.' Almost every hill has one: to the northeast there's a Moorish fort; no fewer than four ruined fortresses guard the harbour entrance; and two more, still in good repair – the **Atalaya** and **Galeras** castles – protect the sea-front arsenal, of vital importance to Spain's military.

Immediately west of the Castillo de la Concepción are the ruins of the 13th-century **Iglesia de Santa María Vieja**. Its Romanesque portal is a 19th-century restoration, but the Roman and Byzantine columns, and Roman mosaic floor, are authentic. In the adjacent Calle del Cañón, look for the **well-head** with weathered rope-marks that traditionally inspired Saint Isidore, the youngest of a sixth-century Visigoth duke's four saintly children, to argue the merits of perseverance.

Still near the centre, the Museo Nacional de Arqueología Marítima on Calle Dique de Navidad has shipwreck finds and a replica of a Roman gallery.

Quite a long trek to the northwest is the **Museo Arqueológico**, noted for its exceptional collection of Roman mining tools used to extract the considerable mineral wealth of nearby La Unión town.

Although the Costa Cálida extending southwest beyond Cartagena has opened up to property development, you can still find quieter stretches of beach. But don't be tempted to camp – camping on the beaches will result in a hefty fine throughout Spain.

The first stop is **Puerto de Mazarrón**, 34km (21 miles) west of Cartagena. The spacious beaches

> **Mileage of cars is calculated in litres per 100 kilometres.**

here have long been patronised by the Spanish. Now all of Europe has caught on. You'll know **Águilas**, a town of 23,000 people about 50km (30 miles) further west, by its 16th-century castle, which dominates the area. The town has a wide sandy bay and, to the north, swimming from the rocks around Cabo Cope. To the south lie several attractive and relatively quiet beaches.

The N-332 now strikes inland for 32km (19 miles) to the small town of **Cuevas de Almanzora**, in a hilly region once inhabited by Stone Age man. Many of the numerous caves hereabouts (from which the town takes its name) are inhabited by local gypsies.

Follow the N-332 a little further to **Vera**, then take the road to **Garrucha** and the coast (the N-340 continues inland until Almería). There are 10km (6 miles) of wild, rocky beaches with a dramatic mountain backdrop. About 5km

(3 miles) south brings you to thriving **Mojácar**, a village planted on the eastern extremity of the rugged Sierra Cabrera. Around 3,000 years ago, the town was an important Phoenician port, but earthquakes and major geological upheavals have left it high and dry. For centuries the women of Mojácar were kept behind the veil, and the place is still known as the 'Village of the Covered Ones'. It is also known as the 'Village of Witches' deriving from Mojácar's long and continuing flirtation with faith heal-

Mojácar, a village characterised by steep hillsides dotted with whitewashed cube houses.

ing, spells and magic brews. This picturesque town is the last bastion of the mystical sign of the *Indalo,* a figure holding a rainbow over his head that was believed to be a talisman against the evil eye. Nowadays, you are more likely to see the *Indalo* in the form of a lucky charm on sale in souvenir shops rather than painted, as it once was, on house doors.

Despite the increasing number of foreign residents, Mojácar is a charming small town with some lovely beaches and good restaurants. It is also rumoured to be the birthplace of Walt Disney – but that's another story.

The narrow coastal road continues another 22km (14 miles) weaving through a moody landscape of barren mountains to **Carboneras**. The long sandy beaches along this stretch of coastline provide another favourite spot for sunbathing and swimming.

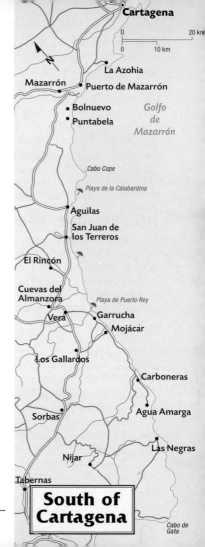

South of Cartagena

From Carboneras, the road continues 41km (25 miles) inland through sweeping, treeless moorland to **Níjar**. This pleasant Andalusian hilltop village is a busy centre for potters, and the narrow streets of the old town centre invite exploration. Look out for local ceramics with their characteristic design of tiger stripes and splashes – the colours are allowed to run deliberately to create the effect.

> While driving on winding mountain roads, it's advisable to sound your horn.

Lying south of Nijar, spectacular cliffs and isolated beaches mark the hard-to-reach natural park of the **Cabo de Gata**.

THE MOORISH LEGACY INLAND

Four historic towns – Elche, Crevillente, Orihuela and Murcia – line the N-340 from Alicante. The most distant of them, Murcia, is only about 80km (48 miles) away and all four can be visited in a couple of days. While these towns have been influenced by various cultures, the Moorish legacy is predominant in each.

Elche

Thousands upon thousands of date palms overwhelm the eye in Elche, a city as old as the Iberians and a UNESCO World Heritage Site. The trees, originally planted by the Carthaginians in 300BC, thrive under irrigation. They still stand as the Moors described them, with 'feet in water, heads in the fire of heaven'. Elche's palms are watered by Abderraman III's 10th-century irrigation system and surround the town of some 200,000 inhabitants on three sides.

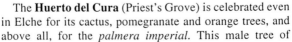

The **Huerto del Cura** (Priest's Grove) is celebrated even in Elche for its cactus, pomegranate and orange trees, and above all, for the *palmera imperial*. This male tree of exceptional age and size has seven branches growing from one main trunk. The *palmera imperial* and many other trees in the grove have been dedicated to royalty and celebrities such as Carmen Polo de Franco, the widow of the Generalísimo.

Overlooking the grove's lily pond is an exact replica of the famous bust of the *Dama de Elche* (The Lady of Elche). The original, dating from 500BC and now housed in Madrid's Archaeological Museum, remains something of a puzzle almost 100 years after it

Fascinating plant life draws many to the town of Elche, a city as old as the Iberians.

came to light. If you look beyond the exotic headdress, you'll see why attributions are difficult to make: the face could be male or female, Spanish, Greek or Eastern.

To visit the place where the bust was discovered, go to the nearby hamlet of **La Alcudia**. Be sure to see the exhibits of Iberian and Roman finds displayed in the excellent local museum.

On the way, you'll see palms that look rather like giant asparagus tips. *Encapuchadores* bind these male trees in spring to produce the pale bleached fronds that are used in Palm Sunday celebrations. These branches, once suitably blessed, are said to conduct lightning, and you'll see them attached to houses all over Spain. The female palms make a less esoteric annual contribution of 10,000 tons of dates, which ripen in December and are highly prized for their juicy sweetness.

Back in Elche, there are more palm trees to see and more luxuriant tropical foliage to admire. You can dine and dance in the frond-slatted shade of the **Parque Municipal**, which also features citrus trees and a noisy frog pond. Or visit the **Huerta de Baix** and the **Huerto del Chocolater** (the latter open at irregular intervals) – these groves help to make Elche one of the most verdant cities in Europe.

Not far from the Municipal Park, the **Calahorra Tower**, 'Guardian of Elche,' once formed part of the main gate in the long-vanished wall that surrounded Elche in Moorish times.

Next to the tower you'll see the blue dome of the **Iglesia de Santa María**. The church was built in the 17th century

Royal Palms

Two date palms in the Huerto del Cura supply the Spanish royal household with fruit. The specially chosen trees were dedicated to Spain's reigning monarchs, King Juan Carlos and Queen Sophia, during a traditional ceremony they attended in 1977.

The palms were first watered with wine by the King and Queen. Signs with the names of the monarchs were then hung on the trees by caretakers, who scaled the slippery trunks to cut bunches of dates for the royal couple to sample.

Theirs aren't the only palms with a royal pedigree. The famous *palmera imperial* was dedicated to Empress Elizabeth of Austria during the visit she made to the grove in 1894. Another tree provided Otto of Austria and Hungary with dates. With more than a thousand palms, many of them over 200 years old, the Huerto del Cura is a noble sight, even by royal standards.

A replica of the famous Dama de Elche overlooks the lily-pond in Elche's Priest's Grove.

and rebuilt after being damaged during the Civil War. Every August a spectacular form of sacred theatre, *El Misterio de Elche (The Mystery of Elche)*, is performed here by an amateur cast of priests, civic dignitaries, and other local people. The play has been presented in Elche for more than five centuries. The music, Gregorian and traditional, is sung in old *lemosín*. During the rest of the year you can see a multimedia presentation of the play at the **Museo Municipal de la Festa**.

Across the main road from the church you can't miss the solid **Alcázar de la Señoría**, known locally as the Palacio de los Altamira, with its square towers. This Moorish palace formed part of the city wall. In times past, Spanish monarchs such as James the Conqueror and Ferdinand and Is-

– once the town's agricultural labourers – threatened the fertility of Orihuela's crops in 1609, brave townspeople hid away enough converted Moors to ensure a good harvest.

The **old university**, on the northern outskirts of the city, was constructed in the 16th and 17th centuries. It's now a school, the **Colegio de Santo Domingo** (St Dominic's School; open Tues–Sun). The spreading Baroque cloisters, magnificent staircase and beautifully tiled refectory are lovely. Near the school you'll see all that's left of the town's original wall, the **Puerta de la Olma** (Elm Tree Gate).

> When visiting churches, shorts, backless dresses and tank tops should not be worn.

Now make for the Plaza de Caturla, a small square on the western outskirts of Orihuela. From here you can as-

A moment's respite: the Romanesque cloister in Orihuela's impressive cathedral.

cend a hill to the old **Seminario de San Miguel** (Saint Michael's Seminary) which offers panoramic views of Orihuela below and a ruined castle above.

There are many historic buildings to see in Orihuela; the town remains much as it was centuries ago, despite an earthquake in 1829 and present-day industrialisation. The Gothic **cathedral**, begun in the early 14th century, with spiral rib vaulting and ornamental grille-work, is considered one of the region's finest. The **Museo**

This bizarre she-devil sculpture was carved by Nicolas de Busi in 1688.

Diocesano de Arte Sacro (Diocesan Museum of Sacred Art) features a famous painting by Velázquez, called the *Temptation of Saint Thomas Aquinas*. The fine Romanesque **cloister** was moved here from a nearby convent that suffered damage in the Civil War. It was erected around an early Gothic cross that is Orihuela's austere monument to Spain's war dead.

Orihuela's **Museo de Semana Santa** (the Easter Week Museum) features the massive floats by Salzillo and other artists, depicting Biblical scenes with life-like statues. A bizarre curiosity here is the *Paso de la Diablesa* (She-Devil Statue). The ghastly horned face of the devil has been terrifying the irreverent into repentance since 1688, when Nicolas de Busi carved it. Every year the she-devil and her companion, a carved skeleton, are trundled through Orihuela as a 'warning to the wise'.

Murcia

Like Elche and Orihuela, Murcia has been a rich oasis since Moorish times. Its market gardens, second only to Valencia's, are watered by the River Segura and yet another Moorish irrigation system. Today's provincial capital was a favourite city of the Moors and in 1224 they even made it the capital of a small *taifa*, or break-away kingdom.

The most celebrated local hero was the powerful yet benign Cardinal Belluga y Moncada. This warlike prelate thwarted the all-conquering Archduke Charles of Austria in 1707, during the War of the Spanish Succession, preventing Charles from advancing by flooding Murcia's fields, then attacking the invader with a small army recruited at his own expense.

Murcia's cathedral stands on the plaza named in honour of Cardinal Belluga. Construction of the **Catedral de Santa María** (on the site of a mosque) began in 1394. There's not a hint of the 14th century in its splendid western façade, however. This Baroque renovation, one of Jaime Bort's celebrated designs, was undertaken when the

Taking the Waters

For a change from the refreshing sea, you can unwind the way the Romans did, sweating it out in a spa. The area has two important and accessible spas, Archena and Fortuna. They date all the way back to the times of the Moors and the Romans.

Choose either simple public baths where a few euros buy a place for the day (the gossip is free) or expensive private facilities in a hotel such as the one at Archena. This isolated spa occupies a spectacular site in an oasis of towering trees; the waters clearly work for them.

Murcia

original Gothic front suffered irreparable damage in a disastrous flood of the Segura in 1735. You can climb the round tower that rises from the north side of the building. There's an impressive view at the top of its five storeys, which are easily ascended.

Inside the cathedral, the **Capilla de los Vélez** (Chapel of the Vélez) is remarkable for its Plateresque decoration. This highly ornamental style is typical of 16th-century Spain. The *coro* (choir) shelters a *Christ* by Francisco Salzillo, one of many supremely realistic works by this native son of Murcia. Others (a *Saint Jerome* and a *Virgin*) are on display

The splendid western façade of the Catedral de Santa María in Murcia.

among the chalices and *retablos* of the Museo Diocesano, adjoining the cathedral.

Before you leave the sanctuary, visit the **Capilla Mayor** (Main Chapel). The strangest of the cathedral's treasures is contained in an urn here: it is the heart of Alfonso the Wise, bequeathed to Murcia by the 13th-century king long before his death.

Go out of the cathedral on the north side and walk across Plaza Hernandez Amores to the cool and classy **Calle de la Trapería** (Street of Secondhand Merchants). But don't look for bargains here; the name of this pedestrian thoroughfare belies the elegance of its shops.

At the north end you come upon the **Casino** (a private club, not a gambling establishment), with spirited turn-of-the century decor. The entrance hall, an exact copy of the Hall of Ambassadors in Seville's Alcázar, and the ladies' lavatory – with its ceiling of cherubs – are the most magnificent rooms.

During the Casino's heyday, the pedestrian **Calle de la Platería** (Street of Silversmiths), at right angles to the Trapería, was full of practising craftsmen. Flower stalls in the Plaza de las Flores are open every morning. After 11am, vendors tend to retreat into nearby shops and bars, particularly in hot weather.

Northwest of the city centre is the Ermita de Jesús church and its impressive **Museo Salzillo**. The highly important group of sculptures gathered here represents every facet of Francisco Salzillo's work. During a career that spanned the 18th century, Salzillo produced large processional figures still carried in Holy Week celebrations, and small intimate carvings, some of them on a miniature scale. Also worth a visit is the **Museo de Arqueología**, on the Calle Gran Via Alfonso, which traces the history of the region from Roman times.

Waterwheels have been operating in the Murcia region for more than 1,000 years. You can see one at **La Ñora**, 6km (3½ miles) from Murcia city centre. The original wheel has been replaced with a steel one, but the Moorish system is otherwise unchanged. A few kilometres (a couple of miles) further, in the direction of Granada on the N-340, the **Museo de la Huerta** (Agriculture Museum) at **Alcantarilla** adjoins a second waterwheel, also of steel. Museum exhibits present all aspects of Murcian country life, including traditional furnishings.

A contemporary waterwheel and Moorish irrigation system in Murcia.

WHAT TO DO

THE BULLFIGHT

Despite an increasing number of Spaniards who are anti-bullfighting, the *corrida* tradition continues, especially during fiesta time. There are several major bull rings in the Costa Blanca area, including Alicante, Cartagena and Murcia. Top matadors – qualified *toreros* who fight fully grown half-ton bulls–occasionally appear in Benidorm, while novice fighters can be seen in other tourist centres. If you want to visit a bullfight, the best seats to buy are *sol y sombra, tendido bajo,* lower stands in the sun part of the time and in the shade the other. The first two rows are the most expensive. Admission prices are lower in Alicante than in Benidorm. Tickets everywhere are 20 percent more than the official price when purchased from agencies and as much as 40 percent more from hotels. Whether you have booked in advance or not, try to arrive at the *plaza de toros* with an hour to spare, enough time to watch the crowd and feel the tension rising. The *corrida* always starts on time – even if the clock occasionally has to be stopped.

The usual six bulls, fought by three matadors, give an average spectacle of 2½ hours, so a cushion hired on the spot is a good idea.

Each phase of the fight is closely controlled by the *presidente,* from his flag-draped box. He drops two handkerchiefs, one to signal the swaggering parade that precedes the fight, and the other to release the first bull from the *puerta de toriles,* the matador's 'gate of fear', for the opening act or first *tercio.* The bull is played with magenta capes–first by the matador's team, or *cuadrilla,* then by the matador himself. All the time the *torero* is assessing the bull, noting his temperament, how he charges, and how he uses his horns. The *picador's* moment comes during the second *tercio,* when he rides into the ring on a horse protected by padding. His task is to lance the bull's huge shoulder muscles; it's unattractive but necessary, both to weaken the bull and to lower his head for the kill. Too much lance, and the *picador* ruins the fight. Too little, and he gives the *torero* an impossible task.

Now *banderillas* – long, ribboned, steel-tipped darts – are plunged into the bull's shoulders. Then the *banderillero,* or even the matador himself, runs obliquely across the path of the bull, barely pausing as he jack-knifes over the horns to thrust home the darts.

The third and final *tercio* is known as *la suerte de la muerte* or the 'act of death'. The *torero* steps alone into the ring and plays the bull with the small, red cape, or *muleta* – taunting him, calling him, passing those horns within inches of his body. *Olés* and crescendos from the band mean the *matador* is doing well, but if you hear whistles and the cry *¡fuera!* (out!), you'll know he's struggling.

At the moment of highest tension, the *matador* leans over the horns to thrust his sword deep into the bull's aorta for the kill. Success means instant death. But the target, a tiny fist-sized area between the shoulders, can only be reached when the animal's feet are together; and swift kills, which need strength as well as skill and nerve, don't always happen.

If the fight has been good and the kill clean, the *presidente* will award the *torero* one or both of the bull's ears and, for exceptional performances, the tail, too. An ear is usually the signal for a lap of honour and, if the crowd agrees with the award, flowers and *botas* of wine shower into the ring. Very occasionally an exceptional performance by the bull earns him a reprieve for breeding. In this case, the *presidente* drops a green handkerchief and the crowd goes wild. The *corrida* is not for everyone. But see one before you pass judgement on this extraordinary institution.

FOLK DANCING

The best-known traditional dances on the Costa Blanca are the *jota valenciana* and *jota murciana*. Sets of vivacious performers either dance alone facing a partner or in pairs. Their steps can be vigorous or stately and gracious.

The dancers are accompanied by musicians playing the guitar or instruments introduced into the region by the Moors – the *dulzaina* (flute) and *tamboril*

At a **corrida** *in Alicante, a young* **matador** *baits the bull with his cape.*

(tambourine). The rhythms go all the way back to the Iberians and reflect a diversity of influences, from Moorish to Aragonese and Castilian to Cuban.

Both old and young take part, attesting to the growing revival of interest in Spain's rich heritage of traditional dance and music.

FLAMENCO

Guitars, the rhythm of castanets and drumming heels, and taut, anguished songs – that's flamenco. You'll be left breathless by these songs and dances from Andalusia.

There are two distinct forms of flamenco: the *cante jondo* (deep song) is an outpouring of intense, soul-searching emotions. The agonised songs, heavy with the wail of Arabia, come from deep within the singer, while the dances are formal and sombre. *Cante jondo* is seldom heard outside Andalusia and Madrid, except on recordings.

Not so the *cante chico* (light song), a more animated version performed in *tablaos* (floor shows) on the Costa Blanca. With a little luck, you may even see flamenco performed by a top Spanish dance company touring on behalf of the Ministry of Information and Tourism's *Festivales de España*. Although the songs may express something of the *cante jondo's* desolation, the dancing is very different. The *fandango, tango, farruca* and *zambra* are performed to the staccato rhythm of *palmadas* (hand-clapping), *pitos* (finger-snapping), the *zapateado* of fiercely drumming heels, and the fiery compulsion of the castanets.

In the *tablaos* and on the stage, the women, their hair swept severely back, swirl in flounced and flowing tight-waisted dresses. The men perform in the Cordoban suit – slightly flared, high-waisted trousers, frilled shirt and short jacket. These traditional costumes, and the fervent pride of the performers who wear them, make for a colourful spectacle without equal on the cabaret stage.

FESTIVALS

There are so many religious and folk celebrations on the Costa Blanca that you are bound to see one whenever you go *(see pages 76–7 for a selection of major events)*. Dates are changeable, so check with the Spanish National Tourist Office in your country or, better still, with the local office in Spain.

SPORTS AND RECREATION

Beaches and Swimming

Much of your Costa Blanca holiday will be spent on the beaches – and there are hundreds of them to choose from. Some slope gently and are thronged with people; others are

Young folk dancers perform traditional dances in the streets.

FESTIVALS

March or April

General, especially
Cartagena (fluctuates)

Semana Santa (Holy Week): major
nationwide week-long Easter celebrations; deeply religious and often
lavishly costumed.

Murcia (fluctuates)

Fiesta de la Primavera (Spring Festival): folklore and fantasy, parades,
fireworks and fanfares begin the
week following Holy Week.

April

Alcoy (fluctuates)

Moros y Cristianos (Moors and Christians): brilliantly costumed parade
and sham battle held on or about
Saint George's Day.

Alicante (fluctuates)

Semana Mediterránea de la Música
(Classical Music Festival): top performers and orchestras.

June

Alicante (the week
including the 24th)

Hogueras de San Juan (Saint John's
Eve): similar to *las Fallas* in Valencia
with fireworks and satirical effigies
set alight in the streets, plus parades
and bullfights.

July

Coastal resorts
(Torrevieja, Santa

Virgen del Carmen: said to bring
luck to the year's fishing; an effigy of

Pola, etc – 16 July)	the *Virgen* is taken out to sea for a blessing, surrounded by fishing boats. Followed by fireworks on the beach.
Benidorm	*Festival Español de la Canción* (Song Festival): major Spanish song festival.
Villajoyosa (24–31 July)	*Moros y Cristianos* (Moors and Christians): Costa Blanca's most spectacular local historical pageant; *see page 35*.
Mar Menor (end-July–mid-August)	Various regattas.

August–September

Torrevieja	*Festival de Habaneras*: see page 50.
Elche (13–15 August)	*Misterio de Elche* (Elche mystery play): performed in two parts on 14 and 15 August, preceded by a public dress rehearsal of both parts on 13 August.
Játiva (15–20 August)	*Gran Feria de Játiva*: originally a horse fair dating from 1250; now includes general festivities, especially *Día del Turista* (Tourist's Day).
Denia and Jávea (fluctuates)	*Moros y Cristianos*: Moors and Christians come in from the sea and battle ensues, resulting in the Moors being driven back.
Bocairente (29 August–2 September)	*Fiesta de Danza Folklórica* (Folk dance Festival) *Día de San Agustín*.

tucked away in coves beneath spectacular cliffs, assuring all the privacy and tranquillity of a desert island *(see* BEACHES, *page 101).*

Like resorts elsewhere in the Mediterranean, those on the Costa Blanca have no lifeguards. There are Red Cross offices on the most popular beaches but, other than that, you're on your own. Flags are used at all beaches to advise swimmers of sea conditions: a green flag means the sea is safe for swimming, while a red flag warns of danger. Normal precautions apply here as elsewhere: beware especially of water-skiers and jet-skis, which sometimes stray from their flagged areas.

Most of the beaches with fine sand are to the north of Alicante. In general, these have been developed as resorts and offer all sorts of facilities – everything from speedboats and parasails to deck chairs and sunshades. The further south you go, the fewer provisions you'll find for water-related activities. The beaches towards the south can be pebbly,

Hardly a sleepy village, Benidorm caters for thousands of international tourists every year.

San Juan's endless stretch of azure-coloured sea and sparkling white sand makes it the perfect holiday spot.

while the sand is usually coarse. But the area beyond Cartagena remains largely uncrowded; people are rare on this stretch of coast, so if you're not looking for companionship this is the place to enjoy a solitude disturbed only by the crash of waves on the shore.

Away from the beach, there's swimming at Benidorm's Aqualandia Verano, a water fun park.

Snorkelling and Scuba Diving

For a new perspective on the wonders of the deep, all you need is a mask and breathing tube; the fins are optional. Snorkelling is at its best off cliffs and near rocks. Offshore, snorkellers are required, for safety reasons, to tow a marker buoy.

For more profound sea experiences, try scuba diving. Several centres provide equipment, a dive boat, expert local knowledge, and sometimes tuition as well. A diving permit is required under Spanish law. Unless you speak reasonable Spanish and know where to go, let your chosen diving centre deal with the documentation. Diving is virtually always safe:

the rips, currents, tides and giant predators found in other seas scarcely exist here.

All cliffs and islands, including Benidorm's small reef, offer interesting diving. Local experts will show you where to find air-locked caves, probe modern wrecks full of surprises, or watch a fresh-water spring bubble mistily from the seabed.

The waters around Calpe's Peñón have a tremendous variety of sea life such as the big-mouthed grouper, the rare zebra-striped bream, and the Turkish wrasse. Any archaeological finds (and they are rare) must be handed in to the Comandancia de Marina.

Boating

Most beaches offer boats for hire, but the only resorts with a variety of craft to choose from are on the Mar Menor. Benidorm is usually the most expensive resort.

You can take out a pedal boat, a stable two-seater propelled by a bicycle-like waterwheel (young children should be accompanied). *Gondolas* – open, banana-shaped boats powered by a double-ended paddle – are not suitable for small children. Although many of the larger beaches have a few

Discussing rates for boat hire in Benidorm: most beaches offer boats for hire by the hour or day.

assorted sailing boats for hire, La Manga is the place to go for the keen sailor.

Windsurfing and Kite-Surfing

Kite-surfing has rapidly become as popular as windsurfing throughout Spain's *costas* and there are several outfits on the Costa Blanca that hire out equipment for both sports, as well as offer vital tuition.

Water-Skiing

Rising fuel costs mean that water-skiing is becoming an expensive sport; all the more reason to double-check rival schools for length of runs, number of attempts allowed for 'getting up,' and discounts for multiple runs. Serious lessons are usually confined to the early morning, when the sea is

calmest. For something less energetic, try parasailing (powerboat parachuting). You needn't even get your feet wet, and the views are superb.

Fishing

The rivers of the Costa Blanca region may reveal carp and barbel, but don't expect much excitement. The best fresh-water fishing hereabouts is the Amadorio Dam, 4km (2½ miles) from Villajoyosa *(see page 33)* and, to a lesser extent, Guadalest's dam. They hold barbel, the biggest carp, small-ish black bass, and rainbow trout – introduced in 1977 and still protected. To catch them you'll need a licence with a trout supplement. The season for non-mountain trout runs from the first Sunday in March to 15 August. The Ministry of Agriculture and Fisheries oversees licences.

If you go sea fishing, you will need local knowledge to hook big grey mullet, sea bream, bass and maybe even grouper below quiet cliffs, and mackerel two or three miles out. In summer, you may catch the tasty dorada; in late summer, autumn and winter, various species of tuna and swordfish.

Tennis

A hotel court will probably be your best chance for a game of tennis, but it may not be possible to hire balls and racquets. La Manga has more than 30 courts, including a tennis club.

Golf

Although the golf courses on the Costa Blanca are open to visitors, you should book in advance. Clubs, caddies and, occasionally, electric trolleys can be hired. The two 18-hole Kentucky blue-grass courses near La Manga are the region's lushest, with shady palms. There is also a fine 18-hole course at Torrevieja's Club Villa Martín and three good nine-hole courses: Altea-la-Vieja's Don Cayo, where the hills test legs as well as golfing skills, the San Jaime Club de Ifach between Calpe and Moraira, and the Club de Golf in Jávea.

Horse Riding

For centuries, horse riding has been a Spanish speciality. There are ranches that cater for the tourist trade and provide a quiet seaside jog. Other centres offer good horses, skilled instruction and interesting cross-country riding. Inexperienced riders can enjoy a moonlight excursion, with a barbecue at the end of an easy ride – an excellent way to meet people.

For the experienced and saddle-fit, there are mountain treks of up to five days, for instance via Altea's Río Algar, or

The Costa Blanca offers several fine golf courses, all of which are open to visitors.

from La Sella, near La Jara. These treks go through orange, almond and olive groves, across rivers and up through pine forests and open moors to real sierra country.

Bird-Watching

Ornithologists, bring your binoculars. The Costa Blanca is crossed by principal migration routes and holds considerable, often unsuspected, bird life. In summer, if you sit by any reasonably quiet estuary, you may see black tern.

In autumn and winter, bird-watchers search cliffs, particularly Calpe's Peñón, for the rare Audouin's Gull: look out for a small, sleek 'herring gull' with dark-olive legs and a heavyish red bill banded in black.

In winter, the Salinas de la Mata, just south of Guardamar, often (but not always) attracts thousands of migratory flamingos, a few of which sometimes stay to breed.

Hunting and Shooting

Spain has always been rich in hunting and shooting possibilities, from wolf to wild boar – though the Costa Blanca is hardly the place for it. Tourist offices have a brochure, 'Caza', which gives more information about where to go for good hunting and how to obtain the necessary permits.

SHOPPING

You will often find the Costa Blanca's best buys off the main streets or in the markets. For the greatest variety and lowest overall prices, shop in the side streets of Alicante. For special items, go inland to the place of manufacture, keeping in mind the prices asked on the coast and at home: Guadalest for ponchos and shawls; Gata for cane, basket work and guitars; Crevillente for woven rugs and carpets; Jijona for *turrón;* Ibi for toys.

In general, look for good prices at hypermarkets outside the major towns.

Save your bargaining for the gypsies and antique dealers, but remember that they have been at it a long time. Beware of *rebajas* (sales); they may be genuine, but reductions are generally few and far between, especially in season.

The Spanish government levies a value-added tax (called IVA) on most items. Tourists from overseas can get a refund on the IVA they have paid on purchases over a stipulated amount. Major tourist shops have forms and details. The refund eventually arrives at your home address.

Summer shopping hours are generally from 10am to 2pm and from 5pm to 8pm (during the rest of the year shops open later and close earlier). The big Alicante and Valencia department stores stay open during the traditional *siesta,* which is the quietest time to shop. In the tourist season, small shops

The product and the process: a local craftswoman makes shawls at her stall in the market.

often stay open on a Saturday evening and Sunday morning. Bakeries and newsagents open in the morning only on most *fiestas* – but don't count on it.

A chemist's is called a *farmacia* (fahrmah-thyah), and all towns and villages will have a 24-hr duty chemist within close vicinity, with details posted on every *farmacia*'s door.

Best Buys

Antiques can be good buys, but beware of fakes. Look for copper and brass, hand-painted tiles and simple oil lamps. If you can find one, and carry it home, buy a traditional cradle. Few are authentically antique, but they are decorative and excellent for holding all sorts of things – even babies.

Cuban cigars are exceptional value for money (but US residents are not allowed to bring them home). Canary Island cigars and locally made cigarettes are even cheaper.

Leather goods are no longer a bargain in Spain, though good quality products may still cost less than at home.

Lladró porcelain has long been a collector's item. The Lladró brothers opened their factory in Tabernes Blanques, near Valencia, in 1958. Opposite is a seconds shop. Less detailed models are sold under the name *Nao*.

Mat and basket-work has been a local craft for 1,500 years and is not very expensive.

Ponchos and knitted shawls from Guadalest are colourful and attractive.

Rugs woven in Crevillente are long-wearing and can be made to your own design.

Souvenirs include pottery, some featuring Moorish designs; bullfight and flamenco posters with your name topping the bill; low-crowned, broad-brimmed Cordoban leather hats; hand-painted fans; elegant *mantillas* (the traditional lace shawls for special occasions); and *botas,* soft leather wine bottles (avoid those with plastic linings).

EATING OUT

Far more interesting than the so-called international cuisine, the hearty local dishes are worth seeking out: ingredients come fresh from the sea or the farm and are served with a wide choice of the region's excellent vegetables. Most tourist hotels and restaurants specialise in caution, with menus guaranteed to cause neither rapture nor complaints. Ask around and find out where Spaniards and resident expatriates eat.

Many restaurants close on Sunday evenings and for a month or two in summer or autumn, so check before going.

Wineskins (botas), *the soft leather wine bottles which make excellent souvenirs.*

Soups and Stews

The favourite dish of many visitors is the Andalusian 'liquid salad,' *gazpacho*. This chilled, tasty soup, based on chopped tomatoes, peppers, cucumbers and garlic, is a rousing refresher on a hot summer day. *Caution: gazpachos with an s is quite a different dish (see page 90).*

Michirones is a splendid mixture of broad beans, chunks of ham, paprika, sausage and hot peppers, plus tasty bits of this and that. *Pebereta talladeta* started life as a stew composed of potatoes, pepper and tuna fish gills, but today thick tuna steaks are often the main ingredient. *Guisado de pavo,* turkey stew, is a gastronomic must: to do justice to this speciality of Orihuela, be sure to order it at least six hours in advance.

Rice and Paella

Excellent rice *(arroz)* has been grown on the Costa Blanca's doorstep since Moorish times; hence the many rice dishes and, king of them all, *paella*. Paella is named after the large, shallow iron pan in which it is cooked and served. The basis is rice, soaked in stock coloured yellow with locally grown saffron, and fried. *Paella valenciana* adds meat, usually crisply fried chicken and pork, and a seasonal variety of peas, green beans, peppers and other vegetables. *Paella alicantina* is the same, plus generous portions of whole prawns, mussels, small whole crabs, octopus and slices of lemon. Vegetarian *paellas* are increasingly available.

> **Enjoy your meal!**
> *Buen provecho*
> **(bwayn provaychoh)**

Spaniards only eat *paella* at midday – often, unbelievably, as part of a four-course meal. A good *paella* is always made to order, usually for a minimum of two people, and takes about 30 minutes to prepare.

Fish and Seafood

The seafood and fish of the Mediterranean provide some of the coast's most memorable meals. A great favourite is *zarzuela de mariscos,* a variation of a Catalan dish, which combines many different ingredients, just like the Spanish operetta from which it takes its name. Shellfish is served with rice in an unlikely but very tasty sauce of olive oil, ground almonds, assorted spices and chocolate, though local cooks sometimes cheat a bit by adding octopus and other shell-less titbits.

Then there is *langosta* – spiny lobster – as succulent and as expensive as ever, and sometimes priced per 100 grammes (be sure to read the menu's small print). *Gambas* are prawns, and *langostinos* the jumbo-sized version. Try them *a la plancha* (grilled), *a la romana* (fried in batter), or *al pil pil* in a hot spicy sauce. *Emperador* (swordfish) is es-

Fresh from the sea to the market: seafood lovers will not be disappointed by the Mediterranean's tasty offerings.

pecially good grilled, and *lenguado* (sole) is delicious in batter, grilled, or sautéed in butter. For something different, try *dorada a la sal:* a whole fish is packed in wet salt, then baked. It comes to the table in a shiny white jacket that is broken when the fish is cut and served.

Vegetarians

Vegetarians are fairly restricted in choice in Spain, although virtually all restaurants will have *tortilla* (potato omelette) and salad on the menu. Other possibilities include *champiñones* (mushrooms, which are generally fried with garlic), *pisto* (similar to ratatouille) and *espárragos* (asparagus).

El menú del día (menu of the day) often offers you a good meal at a fair price.

Meat Dishes

Rice and fish dishes make up a substantial part of the local diet. However, meat is used in regional cooking, though in nothing like the same range and imaginative presentation.

Among local meat specialities is *gazpachos* (with a final *s* to distinguish it from the chilled soup). This lusty, well-spiced Costa Blanca dish consists of pork, chicken, rabbit and snails – and perhaps even a partridge or pigeon. It's stewed in a large frying pan and traditionally eaten on a kind of pancake. *Criadillas* are considered a delicacy: more than one tourist-conscious menu bills them as 'mountain oysters', but they are in fact bulls' testicles. When it's time for a splurge, try *cabrito asado* (roast kid) or *cochinillo* (roast suckling pig). Both treats are expensive but delicious.

Alioli, a garlic-flavoured mayonnaise, accompanies many dishes. It's an excellent piquant speciality of the Costa Blanca region.

Dessert and Fruit

Ice cream, fruit, rice pudding and *flan* (crème caramel) are the most popular desserts. In the summer and early autumn you will be spoiled with an enormous array of fruit. The weekly markets – the best place to buy – are full of strawberries, *nísperos* (a cousin of the lychee), grapes, figs, melons, peaches, apricots, raspberries, pomegranates, grapefruit, lemons, oranges, tangerines, apples, pears and even locally grown bananas, pineapples and dates.

Tapas

A *tapa* is a mouthful of anything that tastes good, and the variety is enormous: smoked mountain ham, spicy sausages, cheese, olives (some as big as pigeon's eggs), sardines, mushrooms, mussels, squid, octopus, meatballs, fried fish, plus sauces and exotic-looking specialities of the house. The name comes from the practice, sadly almost vanished, of providing a free bite with every drink. The titbit was put on a small plate traditionally used to cover the glass and came to be called a *tapa,* which means lid.

Touring *tapas* bars is great fun, especially in a town's old quarter. It can be expensive – certainly more than the cost of an orthodox meal – but do try to devote at least an evening to it. The code is simple: one helping is called a *porción;* a large serving is a *ración;* half as much is known as a *media-ración.*

Breakfast

The Spaniards start the day with *tostada* (toast), a simple roll or the traditional *churro,* a kind of elongated fritter made by pouring a batter-like mixture into a cauldron of hot olive oil. The golden-brown result is traditionally served with hot chocolate for dunking.

In deference to foreign habits, full breakfast *(desayuno completo)* is served at most tourist hotels. This usually consists of fruit juice, coffee, rolls, eggs and perhaps bacon as well. Although oranges grow all around you, freshly squeezed juice is hard to find. Try anyway. Ask for *zumo natural de naranja* (freshly pressed orange juice).

Mermelada means any form of jam. Marmalade lovers should ask for *mermelada de naranja.* If you prefer bitter orange, be sure to specify *naranja amarga.*

Restaurants

The Spanish eat late, but in tourist areas you will be served lunch from 1pm and dinner from 8pm. Bills tend to include tax and service charge, but it is usual to leave a small tip: more than five percent is generous.

Spanish restaurants are classified and priced by a system of forks, with facilities and length of menu more relevant than the quality of the food. Five forks guarantee real comfort, but the food will not necessarily be better than in a two-or three-fork establishment, just more expensive. A bargain *menú del día* (menu of the day) is often proposed. There are restaurants specialising in them, offering three good courses, bread and a jug of very reasonable *vino de la casa* (house wine).

If you are saving up for a special meal, or just economising, fill up on traditional *potajes,* thick soups full of vegetables, in unpretentious restaurants with one fork or none. Spain's golden potato omelette *(tortilla española)* makes another excellent budget meal. To keep costs down, order *vino de la casa* (wine of the house).

Bars and Cafés

Banish the bars and cafés and you'd disconcert the whole of Spain. These establishments are at the centre of the country's

*Drinks, conversation, and mouth-watering snacks –
a perfect evening at this Benidorm tapas bar.*

social life: where workers take an early morning drink and
businessmen negotiate; where old men play cards and
friends meet to watch the world go by from shaded pave-
ment tables. Traditionally, a drink buys a seat for as long as
you want to stay. In areas popular with tourists, though, you
might find the waiter hovering.

Bars are graded from first to third class and charge accord-
ingly; prices always include service, but a small 5 percent tip
is usual. You will pay up to 15 percent more for service at a
table, especially in tourist centres.

Wines and Spirits

Although wines from the north are considered to be Spain's
best, the Costa Blanca's *vino* is very drinkable and very reasonably priced. Look for *Monóvar, Pinosa* and the lighter,

less plentiful *Ricote* (all available in red, rosé or white). Beware of the innocent-looking red *Jumilla*: its 18 percent alcohol content can sneak up on you. Same peril with the strong Alicante dessert wine, 10 drops of which were long reckoned to be one of nature's surest cures. Although the prescribed amount failed to restore France's ageing Louis XIV to health, it might work wonders with a morning-after feeling. Be sure to taste the Costa Blanca's renowned *Moscatel* wine. It's perfect with dessert and preserves all the sweet, distinctive flavour of a Muscat grape.

Try to visit a *bodega,* one of the large wine cellars to be found in towns and most villages. Wine matured in the enormous, dark barrels that line the walls of the older *bodegas* is

Soft lights accentuate the dining mood as dusk falls near Playa de Levante, Benidorm.

not much more expensive than *vino corriente* (ordinary wine) from a modern, million-litre vat. Sample before buying, especially the cheaper wines. They cost less than some mineral waters and will be blended to your taste; containers are extra. Sherry *(jerez)*, a wine fortified with brandy, has been made in Spain for hundreds of years. By the early 18th century, Spain was already exporting it to France. It's hardly surprising, then, that only Spanish sherry can carry the name unlinked with a country of origin.

> The term for a male waiter is *camarero* (cahmah-rayro), while that for a waitress is *camarera* cahmahrayrah).

You will find all the world-famous names on the Costa Blanca, all at reasonable prices. If you are baffled by the choice of sherry available, remember the main types and experiment.

Finos are dry and pale, with a rich bouquet. They are usually taken as aperitifs, particularly *manzanillas,* the driest of all, and *amontillados. Olorosos* (which include the brown and cream varieties) are sweet, heavy and dark, and go well with dessert. Somewhere between the two are the *amorosos.* These are medium dry, light amber in colour, and can be ordered for an aperitif or as a dessert wine. Most can be bought from the barrel, blended to your own taste.

Spanish champagne *(Cava)* is mass-produced and reasonably priced but almost always sweet. For a dry drink, look for the description *brut. Seco* (dry) never really is, and *dulce* is very sweet.

There are other sparkling wines, *vinos espumosos,* which, when served slightly chilled, go down well on a hot day. Spanish brandy is a bit heavy and sweet and bears little resemblance to the best French cognacs, but it is a good, reasonably priced drink. The more expensive varieties are smoother.

Liqueurs abound. Many famous foreign brands (especially French) are made under licence and sell at prices way below those in their home countries. A glance along the shelves of any bar shows the vast range of Spanish liqueurs. They are mostly sweet and often herbal. Try Alicante's *Cantueso,* made since 1867 and still unknown outside the province.

You'll enjoy *sangría,* an iced, hot-weather drink that combines red wine, brandy and mineral water with fruit juice, sliced oranges and other fruit and sugar. *Beware:* it can pack a punch, especially when laced with rough brandy, but you can always dilute *sangría* with soda water and plenty of ice.

Other Drinks

Tea is usually served as a cup of hot (not boiling) water with a teabag in the saucer.

Coffee is very good. Learn the coffee code: *café con leche,* similar to French morning coffee, is half coffee, half milk; *café cortado* is strong and served with a dash of milk; *café solo* is strong and black. Milder instant coffees are often available.

Coffee without caffeine is *descafeinado.*

To Help You Order...

Could we have a table?	**¿Nos puede dar una mesa?**
Do you have a set menu?	**¿Tiene un menú del día?**
I'd like a/an/some...	**Quisiera...**

| beer | **una cerveza** | milk | **leche** |
| bread | **pan** | mineral water | **agua mineral** |

Ripe for the picking: grapes are grown for winemaking.

97

A

ACCOMMODATION *(hotel; alojamiento)*

The Spanish Tourist office offers brochures listing accommodation by area. Before guests take a room they fill out a form showing hotel category, room number and price, and sign it. Breakfast is generally included in the room rate. When you check into your hotel you might have to leave your passport at the reception desk.

Hostal and **Hotel-Residencia:** modest hotels and/or motel, family concerns, also graded by stars.

Pensión: boarding house, few amenities.

Fonda: village inn, clean and unpretentious.

Parador: state-run establishment usually located outside towns. Advance booking essential in season.

I'd like a single/double room.	**Quisiera una habitación sencilla/doble.**
with bath/shower	**con baño/ducha**
What's the rate per night?	**¿Cuál es el precio por noche?**

AIRPORTS *(aeropuerto)*

Alicante Airport, El Altet, handles domestic and international flights. The airport terminal has a restaurant, snack bars, information desks, a currency exchange office, car hire counters, a duty-free shop and a post office (open between 9am and 2pm). The porters' rate is written on a tag on their jacket lapels. Taxis are available, or use the airport bus service (6.30am–9.30pm).

Murcia Airport is 5km (3 miles) from the city (taxis available). Valencia Airport is 8km (5 miles) from the city (taxis available, or bus no 15 makes the journey in 45 minutes).

Where's the bus for …?	**¿De dónde sale el autobús para …?**
What time does the bus leave for …?	**¿A qué hora sale el autobús para …?**
Porter!	**¡Mozo!**

B

BEACHES

The Alicante area

Postiguet: about 1.6km (1 mile) of soft sand; good sports facilities; promenade and cafés alongside.

Albufereta: about 140m (150yd) of fine sand; excellent sports facilities; holiday apartments, cafés and bars.

San Juan/Muchavista: several kilometres of fine sand; good sports facilities; gardens, car park, restaurants and bars nearby.

Towards the north

Campello: 800m (half a mile) of shingle, pebbles and sand with rocky promontories; promenade restaurants and bars.

Poniente (Benidorm): nearly 3km (2 miles) of fine sand adjoining the old town; good sports facilities; a few cafés.

Levante (Benidorm): over 1.6km (1 mile) of fine sand; restaurants, hotels and bars nearby; good sports facilities.

Albir: about 1.6km (1 mile) of pebbly beach; villas, bars and cafés nearby; very good sports facilities.

Olla de Altea: 455m (500yd) of pebbly beach; big hotel; port with marina; sports facilities.

Puerto (Calpe): 140m (150yd) of fine sand with some pebbles; beautiful views of Peñón de Ifach; few sports facilities.

Fosa or Levante (Calpe): nearly 1.6km (1 mile) of fine sand; park nearby; excellent sports facilities.

Fustera (Calpe): some 45m (50yd) of beach between rocks; some seaweed; no sports facilities.

Castillo (Moraira): 90m (100yd) of fine sand between rocky promontories, ruins of castle nearby; fair provision for sports; port with marina; bars and restaurants nearby.

Travel Tips

Shopping bag: loaf of white bread €1.20, 250g butter €2.30, dozen eggs €2, 1kg steak €9–13, 500gm coffee €1.50, 100gm instant coffee €3, 1 litre fruit juice €0.70–1.00, bottle of wine from €3.

Sports: *golf* (per day) green fee from €50; *tennis* court fee €6 per hour, instruction from €10 per hour; *windsurfing* from €12 per hour; *horse riding* from €12 per hour.

Taxi: meters start at around €3. Prices for long distance journeys are usually fixed, so check before starting your journey.

C

CAMPING *(camping)*

There are official campsites along the whole of the coast. Facilities vary, but most have electricity and running water. Some have shops, small playgrounds for children, restaurants, swimming pools and even launderettes. For a complete list of campsites, consult any Spanish National Tourist Office (see TOURIST INFORMATION OFFICES).

May we camp here?	**¿Podemos acampar aquí?**
We have a tent/caravan (trailer).	**Tenemos una tienda de camping/una caravana.**

CAR HIRE *(coches de alquiler)*

There are car hire firms in most resorts and main towns. Rates vary, so check before committing your money; you will probably get a lower rate if you book from outside Spain in advance.

A deposit, as well as an advance payment of the estimated hire charge, is generally required, although holders of major credit cards are normally exempt from this. VAT or sales tax (IVA) will be levied on the total rental charges. When hiring a car, ask for any seasonal deals.

I'd like to hire a car (tomorrow).	**Quisiera alquilar un coche (para mañana).**
for one day/a week	**por un día/una semana**
Please include full insurance coverage	**Haga el favor de incluir el seguro a todo riesgo.**

CHILDREN

The following are a couple of suggestions for outings with the children that parents might enjoy as well:

Aqualandia Verano, Benidorm's popular water theme park, features water slides and swimming pools. It's closed during the winter months.

Safari Park Vergel is situated about 100km (60 miles) from Alicante on the inland road from Vergel to Pego. You'll see many species of animals – even dolphins (in the park's dolphinarium). For children there is mini motocross as well as aquatic scooters, horses, ponies, jumping beds, go-carts, etc.

To find a suitable babysitter, make enquiries at your hotel reception desk. Very few hotels have resident sitters, but most of them will engage one for you. Tourists on a package holiday can make arrangements for babysitting at their travel agency.

Can you get me a babysitter for tonight?	**¿Puede conseguirme una canguro para cuidar los niños esta noche?**

CIGARETTES, CIGARS, TOBACCO (*cigarrillos, puros, tabaco*)

Spanish cigarettes can be made of strong black tobacco (*negro*) or light tobacco (*rubio*). Imported foreign brands are up to three times the price of local makes, though foreign brands produced in Spain under licence can be cheaper than when bought at home. Locally made cigars are cheap and reasonably good. Canary Island cigars are excellent and Cuban cigars are readily available (though US citizens are not allowed to bring them back into the country). Pipe smokers find the local tobacco somewhat rough.

A packet of … /A box of matches, please.	**Un paquete de … /Una caja de cerillas, por favor.**

CLIMATE and CLOTHING

Climate. Obviously summer is the high season on Spain's sunny coasts; this is often the only time the whole family can get away. But if you are able to plan your trip just before or just after the school holidays you'll find that prices are lower and accommodation easier to find. The following charts indicate monthly average temperatures in Alicante. Minimum averages were taken at dawn, maximum averages at midday.

	J	F	M	A	M	J	J	A	S	O	N	D
°C max.	16	17	20	22	26	29	32	32	30	25	21	17
min.	7	6	8	10	13	15	19	20	18	15	10	7
°F max.	61	63	68	72	78	84	90	90	86	77	70	63
min.	45	43	47	50	56	61	66	68	65	59	50	45

Clothing. Whatever you wear for hot summers will be fine for the Costa Blanca. Have a light sweater handy in the evenings. Between November and March it can be extremely cold, sometimes with winds, so always carry a jacket or something warm. Even in August be sure to take jerseys when going to the mountains. When visiting churches, women no longer *have* to cover their heads, but decent dress is certainly expected.

COMMUNICATIONS

Post offices *(correos)* are for mail, telegrams and faxes (ratesheet available for sending and receiving); normally you can't make telephone calls from post offices.

Post office hours: 9am to 1 or 2pm and 4 or 5 to 6 or 7pm, Monday to Friday (but some only open in the morning from 9am to 2pm). Mornings only on Saturday.

Mail: if you don't know in advance where you'll be staying, you can have your mail addressed to the *Lista de Correos* (poste restante or general delivery) in the nearest town. Take your passport along as identification and be prepared to pay a small fee for each letter received. Some post offices limit acceptance of registered mail to certain times. See posted hours.

Postage stamps are also on sale at tobacconists *(tabacos)* and often at hotel desks. Letterboxes are yellow and red.

Internet: internet cafés are widespread. Check at the local tourist office for a list. You can expect to pay approximately €5 for an hour online.

Telephone *(teléfono)*: You can make local and international calls from public telephone booths in the street, from most hotels (often with heavy surcharges) and from some post offices. For international direct dialling, pick up the receiver, wait for the dial tone, then dial 00, wait for a second sound, and dial the country code (UK 44, Canada and US 1), city code (without the initial 0 for the UK) and subscriber's number.

To reverse the charges, ask for *cobro revertido*. For a personal (person-to-person) call, specify *persona a persona*.

Can you get me this number in …?	**¿Puede comunicarme con este número en …?**
Have you received any mail for …?	**¿Ha recibido correo para …?**
A stamp for this letter/postcard, please.	**Por favor, un sello para esta carta/tarjeta.**
express (special delivery)	**urgente**
airmail/ registered	**vía aérea/ certificado**

COMPLAINTS

Try to settle the matter with the establishment first. If you can't, ask for an official complaint forms *(Hoja Oficial de Reclamación)*. The original of this triplicate document should be sent to the regional office of the Ministry of Tourism, one copy remains with the establishment complained against and you keep the third sheet.

The tourist office (the *Oficina Municipal de Información al Consumidor*) or, in really serious cases, the police, should normally be able to give advice.

CONSULATES *(consulado)*

If you get into serious trouble, seek out the British consulate (see below) which helps citizens of all English-speaking countries (Australia, Ireland, New Zealand, South Africa and the US).

British Consulate, Plaza de Calvo Sotelo 1–2, Alicante; tel: (96) 521 6022, fax: (96) 514 0528 <www.ukinspain.com>.

Travel Tips

CONVERSION CHARTS

For fluid and distance measures, see the charts in DRIVING, *page 110*. Spain uses the metric system.

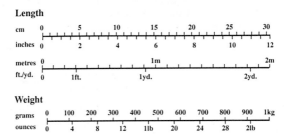

CRIME and THEFT

Spain's crime rate has caught up with the rest of the world. Thefts and break-ins are increasing. Hang on to handbags and wallets, especially in busy places such as at a bullfight, open-air market or fiesta. Don't take valuables to the beach. Lock cars and *never* leave cases, cameras, etc, on view. If you suffer a theft or break-in, report it to the Guardia Civil.

My ticket/wallet/passport has been stolen.	**Me han robado mi billete/ cartera/pasaporte.**

CUSTOMS and ENTRY FORMALITIES *(aduana)*

Most visitors require only a valid passport to visit Spain, but Australian, Canadian, South African and New Zealand citizens should apply for a visa.

Though residents of Europe and North America aren't subject to any health requirements, visitors from further afield should check with a travel agent before departure in case inoculation certificates are called for.

The following chart shows customs allowances for certain items of personal use.

Into:	Cigarettes		Cigars		Tobacco	Spirits		Wine
Spain*	200	or	50	or	250g	1l	or	1l
Australia	200	or	250g	or	250g	1l	or	1l
Canada	200	and	50	and	400g	1.1l	or	1.1l
N Zealand	200	or	50	or	250g	1.1l	and	4.5l
S Africa	400	and	50	and	250g	1l	and	2l
USA	200	and	100	and	**	1l	or	1l
Within EU***	800	and	200	and	1kg	10l	and	90l

*   Arriving from non-EU countries or EU countries with duty-free.
**   A reasonable quantity.
***   Guidelines for non-duty-free within the EU. For the import of larger amounts you must be able to prove that the goods are for your own personal use. For EU duty-free allowances see * above.

Currency restrictions: visitors may bring an unlimited amount of foreign currency into Spain. There is no limit to the amount of Spanish currency brought in or taken out of the country.

I've nothing to declare.	**No tengo nada que declarar.**
It's for my personal use.	**Es para mi uso personal.**

DRIVING IN SPAIN

Entering Spain: to bring your car into Spain you need a valid driver's licence, car registration papers and a Green Card (an extension to your regular insurance policy making it valid for foreign countries).

If you are bringing your own car into Spain, remember that a nationality sticker must be prominently displayed on the back of your car. Seat belts are compulsory, as are crash helmets for scooters or motorbikes. Not using them outside towns makes you liable for a stiff fine.

Travel Tips

(International) Driving Licence	**Carné de conducir (internacional)**
Car registration papers	**Permiso de circulación**
Green Card	**Carta verde**
Full tank, please …	**Llénelo, por favor …**
lead-free/diesel	**sin plomo/diesel**
Check the oil/tyres/battery.	**Por favor, controle el aceite/los neumáticos/ la batería.**
I've had a breakdown.	**Mi coche se ha estropeado.**
There's been an accident.	**Ha habido un accidente.**

E

ELECTRIC CURRENT *(corriente eléctrica)*

Today 220-volt AC is becoming standard (making an adapter necessary for American appliances), but older installations of 125 volts can still be found. Check before plugging in. If the voltage is 125, American appliances (eg razors) built for 60 cycles will run on 50-cycle European current, but more slowly.

If you have trouble with any of your appliances ask your hotel receptionist to recommend an *electricista*.

What's the voltage, 125 or 220?	**¿Cuál es el voltaje, ciento veinticinco (125) o doscientos veinte (220)?**
an adapter/a battery	**un adaptador/una pila**

EMERGENCIES

If you're not staying at a hotel, ring or visit the Municipal Police (091) or the Guardia Civil. If possible, take a Spanish speaker with you, although some police stations now have interpreters in the main tourist areas.

The National Emergency number for Spain is **006**.

Depending on the nature of the emergency, refer to other applicable entries in this book, such as Consulates, Medical Care and Police.

Though we hope you'll never need them, here are a few key words you might like to learn in advance:

Careful	**Cuidado**	Fire	**Fuego**
Help	**Socorro**	Police	**Policía**
Stop	**Deténgase**	Stop thief	**Al ladrón**

GETTING THERE

If you're planning a trip to the Costa Blanca, you should get in touch with a reliable travel agent who has up-to-date information on fares, special tickets and accommodation.

By Air

Scheduled flights

The Costa Blanca is served by Alicante, Valencia and Murcia airports, which are linked by regular flights from the UK and other European cities. The main gateway to Spain is Madrid's Barajas airport.

Charter flights and package tours

From the UK and Ireland: there are charter flights available to the Costa Blanca, generally as part of package tours. It is possible to find your own accommodation and submit this to your travel agent who can then arrange a 'package' with charter flight. Or travel on a charter and use wanderer vouchers to stay in youth hostels, small hotels and the like.

From North America: Barcelona is featured on some Iberian or European packages that let you visit several Spanish cities during a specified period of time. From there, it's possible to hire a car or take the train or bus to Alicante, Murcia and Almería.

Independent travellers

From the UK: airlines with services to the region include British Airways to Alicante, Murcia and Valencia, and Ryan-Air to Murcia.

By Road

The main access road from France to the Costa Blanca is at the eastern side of the Pyrenees via Barcelona on the motorway (ex-

Travel Tips

You're welcome	*De res*	*De nada*
Good-bye	*Adéu*	*Adiós*

Do you speak English?	**¿Habla usted inglés?**
I don't speak Spanish.	**No hablo español.**

LAUNDRY and DRY-CLEANING

Most hotels will handle laundry and dry-cleaning, but they'll usually charge more than a laundry *(lavandería)* or a dry-cleaners *(tintoreria)*. You'll find do-it-yourself launderettes *(launderama)* only in Benidorm.

When will it be ready	**¿Quando estará listo?**
I must have this tomorrow morning.	**Lo necesita para mañana.**

LOST PROPERTY

The first thing to do when you discover you have lost something is to retrace your steps. If nothing comes to light, report the loss to the Municipal Police or the Guardiá Civil.

I've lost my wallet/handbag/ passport.	**He perdido mi cartera/bolso/ pasaporte.**

M

MAPS

Road maps are on sale at most petrol stations, bookshops and news-stands. Road and street signs carry place names both in Castilian and *Valenciano* – a fact not reflected on every map. The most detailed – but not *always* foolproof – cartographic information is contained in the official atlas of Spain (scale 1:400,000), issued by the Ministry of Public Works.

a street plan of ...	**un plano de la ciudad de ...**
a road map of this region	**un mapa de carreteras de esta comarca**

MEDICAL CARE

By far the best solution, to be completely at ease, is to take out a health insurance policy to cover the risk of illness and accident while on holiday.

Health care in the resort areas and in the major cities is good but expensive, hence the need for adequate insurance. However, British visitors can qualify for medical care on the Spanish national health service (get a Form E 111 from your local post office before leaving the UK). For minor ailments, visit the local first-aid post *(casa de socorro* or *dispensario)*. Away from your hotel, don't hesitate to ask the police or a tourist information office for help.

Pharmacies *(farmacia)* are usually open during normal shopping hours. After hours, at least one per town remains open all night, the *farmacia de guardia*. Its location is posted in the window of all other *farmacias*.

I need a doctor/dentist.	**Necesito un médico/dentista.**
I've a pain here.	**Me duele aquí.**
a fever/sunburn	**fiebre/quemadura del sol**
an upset stomach	**molestias de estómago**

MEETING PEOPLE

Politeness and simple courtesies still matter in Spain. A handshake on greeting and leaving is normal. Always begin any conversation with a *buenos días* (good morning) or *buenas tardes* (good afternoon). Always say *adiós* (good-bye) or, at night, *buenas noches* when leaving. *Por favor* (please) should begin all requests.

The Spanish have their own pace. Not only is it bad manners to try to rush them, but unproductive as well.

MONEY MATTERS

Currency: the euro (€) is the official currency used in Spain. Notes are denominated in 5, 10, 20, 50, 100 and 500 euros; coins in 1 and 2 euros and 1, 2, 5, 10, 20 and 50 cents.

Banking hours: 9am to 2pm, Saturdays to 1pm. Outside these hours, currency can usually be changed at a *cambio* or in your hotel. Always take your passport, as it's the only accepted form of identification. Automatic Teller Machines *(telebancos)* are increasingly common, and from them you can draw funds in euros against your bank account with a credit/debit card.

Credit cards: all the internationally recognised cards are accepted by hotels, restaurants and businesses in Spain.

Travellers cheques: in tourist areas, shops and all banks, hotels and travel agencies accept them, though you're likely to get a better exchange rate at a national or regional bank. Always remember to take your passport with you if you expect to cash a travellers cheque.

I want to change some pounds/dollars.	**Quiero cambiar libras/dólares.**
Do you accept travellers cheques?	**¿Acepta usted cheques de viaje?**
Can I pay with this credit card?	**¿Puedo pagar con esta tarjeta de crédito?**

MOSQUITOES

There are rarely more than a few mosquitoes at a given time, but just one can ruin a night's sleep. Few hotels, flats, or villas have mosquito-proofed windows. Bring or buy your own anti-mosquito devices, whether nets, buzzers, lotions, sprays, or incense-type coils that burn all night.

NEWSPAPERS and MAGAZINES *(periódicos; revistas)*

In tourist towns you can buy most European and British newspapers on the day of publication, including the *International Herald Tribune* and *Daily Mail*. Most glossy European and American magazines are available. The *Costa Blanca News* goes on sale on Fridays, and there is a free newspaper, the *Entertainer.*

Have you any English-language newspapers/magazines?	**¿Tienen periódicos/revistas en inglés?**

P

PHOTOGRAPHY

There's tremendous scope for the keen photographer, but beware of the strong light. For good results don't shoot between 11am and 3pm unless there's light cloud to soften the sun.

All popular brands and most sizes of film (except 220) are available. Imported films and chemicals are expensive. Spanish-made film is much less expensive and of a reasonable quality.

Shops in major resorts usually provide a reasonably priced 48- or 72-hour processing service for both black-and-white and colour. It's often safer to develop them at home. If possible always keep film – exposed and unexposed – in a refrigerator.

I'd like a film for this camera.	**Quisiera un carrete para esta máquina.**
a black-and-white film	**un carrete en blanco y negro**
a colour-slide film	**un carrete de diapositivas**
a film for colour pictures	**un carrete para pelicula en color**
35-mm film	**un carrete treinta y cinco**
How long will it take to develop (and print) this film?	**¿Cuánto tardará en revelar (y sacar copias de) este carrete?**

POLICE *(policía)*

There are three police forces in Spain: the *Policía Municipal,* local units in a blue uniform; the *Cuerpo Nacional de Policía,* a national anti-crime unit also in a blue uniform; and the *Guardiá Civil,* the national police force, in a green uniform. Call on any of the three in an emergency.

Where's the nearest police station?	**¿Dónde está la comisaría más cercana?**

PUBLIC HOLIDAYS *(fiesta)*

1 January	*Año Nuevo*	New Year's Day
6 January	*Epifanía*	Epiphany

Travel Tips

1 May	*Día del Trabajo*	Labour Day
25 July	*Santiago Apóstol*	St James' Day
15 August	*Asunción*	Assumption
12 October	*Fiesta Nacional*	National Holiday (Columbus Day)
1 November	*Todos los Santos*	All Saints' Day
6 December	*Día de la Constitución Española*	Constitution Day
25 December	*Navidad*	Christmas Day
Movable dates:	*Jueves Santo*	Maundy Thursday
	Viernes Santo	Good Friday
	Lunes de Pascua	Easter Monday (Catalonia only)
	Corpus Christi	Corpus Christi
	Inmaculada Concepción	Immaculate Conception (normally 8 December)

These are only the national holidays of Spain; 9 October is a local holiday, *Dia de la comunidad valenciana.*

Are you open tomorrow?   **¿Está abierto mañana?**

 R

RADIO and TV *(radio; televisión)*

A short-wave set of reasonable quality will pick up all European capitals. Reception of Britain's BBC World Service is usually poor and often unobtainable along the coast. Onda Cero Internacional (94.6FM) is an English-language station with music, chat and regular BBC news broadcasts. The Spanish music programme, *segundo programa,* jazz to Bach but mostly classical, is excellent. It's FM only, around 88 Mhz on the band.

RELIGIOUS SERVICES

The national religion is Roman Catholicism, but other denominations and faiths are represented. Since 1977 the Costa Blanca has had a permanent English-speaking Protestant chaplain. He functions in various churches and centres, mostly between Benidorm and Denia. The Evangelical Church also has a small but strong following; services, in Spanish, are held regularly. The Synagogue in Benidorm (parque Loix) holds Sabbath services on Friday at 8.30pm. The *Costa Blanca News* carries details of religious services.

SIESTA

A late lunch is often followed by a lengthy nap, usually between 1 and 5pm. Shops re-open at 4 or 5pm until 8 or 9pm.

TIME DIFFERENCES

Spanish time coincides with most of Western Europe – Greenwich Mean Time (GMT) plus one hour. In summer, another hour is added (Daylight Saving Time).

Summer Time chart:

New York	London	**Spain**	Jo'burg	Sydney	Auckland
6am	11am	**noon**	noon	8pm	10pm

What time is it?　　　**¿Qué hora es?**

TIPPING

Since a service charge is normally included in hotel and restaurant bills, tipping is not obligatory. However, it is appropriate to tip hotel porters, petrol-station attendants (for extra services), bullfight ushers, hairdressers and taxi drivers. The chart below gives some suggestions as to what to leave.

Hotel porter, per bag	30 cents
Maid, for extra services	€0.75–1.50
Lavatory attendant	20–30 cents
Waiter	5–10 percent (optional)
Taxi driver	10 percent

Travel Tips

Hairdresser/barber	10 percent
Tourist guide	10 percent

TOILETS

There are many expressions for 'toilets' in Spanish: *aseos, servicios, WC, water* and *retretes*.

Where are the toilets?	**¿Dónde están los servicios?**

TOURIST INFORMATION OFFICES *(oficinas de turismo)*

Spanish National Tourist Offices are maintained throughout the world:

Australia:	Level 2-203 Castlereagh Street, Suite 21A, PO Box 675, NSW, 2000 Sydney South; tel: (2) 264-7966.
Canada:	102 Bloor Street West, 14th floor, Toronto, Ontario M5S–1M9; tel: (416) 961-3131, e-mail: <toronto@tourspain.es>
UK:	22–23 Manchester Square, London W1M 5AP; tel: 020 7486 8077, fax: 020 7486 8034, e-mail: <londres@tourspain.es>
USA:	Suite 915 East 845, North Michigan Avenue, Chicago, IL 60601; tel: (312) 642-1992. 8383 Wilshire Boulevard, Suite 960, Beverly Hills, CA 90211; tel: (213) 658-7188/93. 666 Fifth Avenue, New York, NY 10103; tel: (212) 265-8822, e-mail: <oetny@tourspain.es> 1221 Brickell Avenue, Miami, FL 33131; tel: (305) 358 1992.

These offices will supply you with a wide range of colourful and informative brochures and maps in English on the various towns and regions in Spain. They will also let you consult a copy of the master directory of hotels in Spain, listing all facilities and prices.

All major cities and leading resorts in Spain have their own extremely helpful tourist information offices, all of which will be delighted to provide you with information and brochures on local tourist attractions.

TRANSPORT

Buses: there are good bus services from the Alicante terminal to most towns in the province and further afield, usually every hour. Book your ticket from the relevant kiosk inside the hall. The various companies almost always put on sufficient buses to take waiting passengers, so make sure you get the right one; ie, don't get on the first bus if your ticket says 'Autobús 2'. If you've got a ticket, you've got a bus.

Outside Alicante enquire about bus routes and times at the local tourist office, travel agency, or hotel or, in some towns, at the bus terminal *(estación central de autobuses)*. Most coastal routes are hourly and reasonably regular. Don't worry unduly if the first bus shoots past full up; there will almost certainly be back-up buses behind. Most towns have their own internal services, usually small buses that buzz from beach to beach. Start looking for the last bus about 8pm. Buses are more expensive than the narrow-gauge railway *(see below)*, but less expensive than main line trains.

Taxis: Spain's taxis compare very favourably to those in the rest of Europe. Wherever you're going, with or without a meter, check the approximate fare *before* setting off. If you travel outside a town, you'll be charged the two-way trip unless there is a return fare. Except in Benidorm and Alicante, taxis tend to disappear around midnight, earlier out of season. Arrange to be collected or you may find yourself stranded. By Spanish law taxis may only take four persons per vehicle (although some are willing to risk a fifth if it is a baby or child).

A green light and/or a *Libre* ('Free') sign indicates a taxi is available.

Trains *(tren)*: a narrow-gauge line runs from Alicante to Denia, taking about 2 hours 15 minutes, as the train makes frequent stops. From Alicante, main line trains reach to most corners of Spain. Local trains are slow, stopping at most stations. Long-distance services are fast and punctual. First-class coaches are comfortable, second-class, adequate. Tickets can be purchased at travel agencies as well as at the stations *(estación de ferrocarril)*. For long trips, seat reservations are advisable on most Spanish trains.

class and comfort for the price. Ask for an exterior room where you can sit on the balcony and watch the evening *paseo*. 49 rooms. Major credit cards.

Hotel Bahia Blanca €€ *Cabo la Huerta; tel/fax: (96) 516 0037*. Lovely garden and swimming pool. Dogs allowed in rooms. 16 rooms. Major credit cards.

Mediterránea Plaza €€€€ *Plaza de Ayuntamiento 6; tel: (96) 521 0188, <www.hotelmediterraneaplaza.com>*. A stylish hotel with lots of shiny marble and an excellent restaurant, in a superb position across from the town hall. 50 rooms. Major credit cards.

Hotel Tryp Gran Sol €€€€ *Rambla Méndez Núñez 3; tel: (96) 520 3000, fax (96) 521 1439, <www.solmelia.com>*. If you can look beyond the dated 1970s' style décor, you'll find that this hotel is well located and comfortable. Includes a panoramic lounge on the 26th floor. 80 suites, 43 double rooms. Major credit cards.

Les Monges €€ *Calle Monges 2; tel: (96) 521 5046, fax (96) 514 7189, <www.lesmonges.net>*. This hotel is a real find. It has arty, yet comfortable decor, and rooms include TV, air conditioning, private basins, hairdryers and even piped music. 8 rooms. Major credit cards.

Hotel La Reforma €€€ *Reyes Católicos 7; tel: (96) 592 8147, fax (96) 592 3950*. A very modern hotel. Rooms equipped with TV, air-conditioning, en suite bath and phone. 52 rooms.

Hotel Sol Alicante €€€ *Calle Gravina 9; tel: (96) 521 0700, fax (96) 521 0976*. Another modern hotel, with a view. Parking is an additional €8. 76 rooms. Major credit cards.

ALTEA

Hostal Trovador €€ *Partida Cap Negret 15; tel: (96) 584 1275, fax (96) 688 1309.* Located outside the city, towards the beach. Dogs allowed in rooms. Car park. 15 rooms. Major credit cards.

Hotel Altaya €€€ *La Mar 115; tel: (96) 584 0800, fax (96) 584 0659, <www.hotelaltaya.com>.* Centrally located with a large terrace. Picturesque view from rooms. Parking available. 24 rooms. Major credit cards.

Hotel Cap Negret €€€ *Ptda. Cap Negret 7; tel: (96) 584 1200, fax (96) 584 1600, <www.hotelcapnegret.com>.* A large deluxe hotel with many modern conveniences, including hairdryers, children's playground, bar/disco and swimming pool. Money exchange available. 250 rooms. Major credit cards.

Hotel Apartments Galetamar €€€ *La Caleta 28; tel: (96) 583 2311, fax (96) 583 2328, <www.galetamar.com>.* Rooms have a good view of the beach. Some come equipped with a lounge area and piped radio music. Walking distance from the Playa Levante pedestrianised promenade. The heated swimming pools (for adults and children) are a pleasant alternative to beach bathing. 113 rooms. Major credit cards.

Hotel San Miguel €€ *Calle La Mar 65; tel: and fax (96) 584 0400.* This hotel is located on the beach, so ask for a room with a sea view. Small private bathrooms. Two restaurants both offer a seafood menu for about €12 per meal. The *paella* comes highly recommended. 24 rooms. Major credit cards. Closed November.

Recommended Hotels

BENIDORM

Hostal Benidorm Plaza €€€€ *Via Emilio Ortuño 18; tel: (96) 585 1549, fax (96) 585 2236.* This modern large hotel is in a convenient central location. Sauna, gym, swimming pool and 24-hour room service available. 226 rooms. Major credit cards.

Hostal Lope de Vega €€€ *Severo Ochoa 9; tel: (96) 585 4150, fax (96) 586 7943.* Nice, family-orientated hotel with nursery, heated pool and children's playground. Tennis courts, sauna. Lift. 129 rooms. Major credit cards. Open Easter and summer only.

Hotel Montemar €€€ *San Pedro 18; tel: (96) 585 0600, fax (96) 585 0411.* Centrally located, with wonderful view from rooms. Typical conveniences. Exceptional garden. 97 rooms. Major credit cards. Closed December–February.

Hotel Rambla €€ *Atocha 10; tel: (96) 585 2337, fax (96) 586 2970.* Garden with swimming pool. Coffee bar attached to hotel. Major credit cards. Closed November–Easter.

CALPE

Galetamar €€ *La Caleta 28; tel: (96) 583 2311, <www.gale tamar.com>.* Modern hotel with all mod cons, plus family rooms and bungalows. 33 rooms. Major credit cards.

Pensión Centrica € *Plaza de Ifach; tel/fax: (96) 583 5528.* Intimate, private pensión run for 10 years by a friendly Englishwoman. Pleasant, attractive rooms for a reasonable price. 13 rooms. Major credit cards.

Venta La Chata €€ *Carretera N-332, 172km; tel: (96) 583 0308.* Atmospheric lodging in a 200-year-old country house with both sea and mountain views. Beautiful garden and tennis courts. Coffee-bar. Dogs allowed in rooms. 17 rooms. Major credit cards.

Hotel Roca Esmeralda €€€ *Ponent 1; tel: (96) 583 6101, fax (96) 583 6004, <www.unitursa.com>*. Large hotel, located on the beach. Facilities include hair salon, gymnasium, sauna/Jacuzzi and three outdoor swimming pools. Entrance accessible for guests with disabilities. Bicycles for hire. 212 rooms. Major credit cards.

DENIA

Hostal El Comercio €€ *Calle de La Via; Tel/fax: (96) 578 0071*. Inexpensive but well-equipped. Rooms have bathrooms, TV and phone. 35 rooms.

Hostal Patricia €€ *Fontanella 18; tel: (96) 642 3646*. Centrally located and pleasant. Dogs allowed in rooms. 6 rooms.

Hostal Romano €€€ *Partida les Rotes 71; tel: (96) 578 0323, fax (96) 578 7340*. Set in an ideal location, in a historic building. Ambient music is piped into the lovely rooms. There is a garden on the property. Conveniences include hairdryers in all rooms. Medical services available. 6 rooms. Major credit cards.

Hotel Costa Blanca €€ *Calle Pintor Llorens 3; tel: (96) 578 0336, fax (96) 578 3027, <www.hotelcostablanca.com>*. A comfortable spic-and-span hotel, located conveniently across from the railway station. 54 rooms. Major credit cards.

GANDIA

Bayren €€€ *Paseo Neptuno 62; tel: (96) 284 0300, <www.hotelesbayren.com>*. Lovely hotel on the beachfront with sea views and balconies. 172 rooms. Major credit cards.

Recommended Hotels

Hostal Fin de Semana €€ *Calle Mire Nostrum 45; tel: (96) 284 0097.* Intimate and charming, this guest-house is a wonderful find at a great price. Located on the beach. 15 rooms. Major credit cards.

Hostal Residencia Duque Carlos €€ *Duque Carlos de Borja 34–36; tel: (96) 287 2844.* Reasonably priced, comfortable modern hotel in a convenient central location. 19 rooms. No credit cards.

Hotel Tres Anglas €€€ *Valldigna 11; tel: (96) 284 0266, fax (96) 284 0347, <www.hoteltresanglas.com>.* Very large modern hotel with facilities including a swimming pool, tennis courts, mini-golf and children's playground. Ideally suited for travellers with disabilities with lift and wheelchair-accessible entrances. Medical services are also available. 333 rooms. Major credit cards.

Hostal El Nido €€ *Calle Alcoy 22, Playa de Gandia; tel: (96) 284 4640, fax (96) 284 6571.* A large beachfront *hostal* with comfortable, pleasant rooms and a superb French restaurant. 10 rooms. Major credit cards.

JAVEA

Hostal La Marina €€€ *Avenida de la Marina Española 8; tel: (96) 579 3139, e-mail: pensionlamarina@hotmail.com.* Expensive but well-run hotel with rooms featuring beautiful, sweeping views of the sea. 14 rooms. Major credit cards. Closed November–February.

Hotel Miramar €€€ *Plaza Almirante Bastarrece 12; tel: (96) 579 0102.* This renovated hotel offers comfortable rooms with en-suite bathrooms, phone and TV. 26 rooms. Major credit cards.

SANTA POLA

Hostal Michel €€ *Calle Felipe 11; tel: (96) 541 1842, <www.hostalmichel.com>*. Refurbished rooms with private bathrooms. Friendly service and good restaurant. 24 rooms. Major credit cards.

Hostal Picola €€ *Calle Alicante 64; tel: (96) 541 1868, fax (96) 541 1044*. Slightly more expensive than the average, but a very good *hostal*, so worth paying the extra for. 20 rooms. Major credit cards.

Hotel Polamar €€€ *Playa Levante; tel: (96) 541 3200, fax (96) 541 3183*. Large, standard beachfront hotel. You need to request a sea view room if you wish to have one. 76 rooms. Major credit cards.

TORREVIEJA

Hostal Reina € *Avenida Dr. Gregorio Marañón 22; tel: (96) 670 1904*. Inexpensive and none too comfortable, but very friendly. You may need ear plugs on a Saturday night because of the location on the main road. 14 rooms. No credit cards.

Hotel Cano €€ *Calle Zoa 53; tel: (96) 670 0958, fax (96) 571 9126*. A modern hotel located conveniently close to the bus station. 28 rooms. Major credit cards.

Hotel Fontana €€€ *Rambla de Juan Mateo 19; tel: (96) 670 1125, fax (96) 571 4450, <www.hotelfontana.com>*. Fancy, upmarket hotel located two blocks from the tourist office. 156 rooms. Major credit cards.

Hotel Masa International €€€ *Avenida Alfredo Nobel; tel: (96) 692 1537, e-mail: hotel-masa@arrakis.es*. Lovely clifftop hotel away from the bustle of town. There's a pool, sauna and parking. 50 rooms. Major credit cards.

Recommended Restaurants

We appreciated the food and service in the restaurants listed below (alphabetically, and according to similar town categories as for the hotels – *see page 126*); if you find other places worth recommending, we would be pleased to hear from you. Our choices often concentrate on restaurants serving local cuisine. You will also find some wonderful restaurants serving a more international style cuisine. They are likely to be attached to the hotel you're staying at. Many hotel owners are native Europeans and have brought their traditional cuisine with them.

As for hotel rooms, meal prices may vary in and out of season (higher during July and August), but by and large they remain within our rating categories, based on the cost of dinner for two, not including drinks:

€ under 35 euros

€€ 35–60 euros

€€€ over 60 euros

Some restaurants close one day a week, some open only for dinner, again with seasonal variations.

ALICANTE

L'Ampadini €€ *Tucuman 6; tel: (96) 512 07 06.* International cuisine, specialising in Greek *moussaka* and homemade desserts. Special menu offered on Thursday, when you can order from a selection of fabulous Canary Island-style dishes prepared to perfection.

Auberge de France €€€ *Flora de España 32; tel: (96) 526 06 02.* Mediterranean and French cuisine are served at this upmarket restaurant. Closed on Monday and Sunday between October and March .

Chino Pekin € *Reyes Catolicos 57; tel: (96) 592 98 67*. If you are seeking a different meal from the typical Alicante-style that is readily available in the area, try this excellent Chinese restaurant. Inexpensive, tasty dishes.

Darsena €€€+ *Marina Deportiva, Muelle 6; tel: (96) 520 75 89*. Elegant restaurant serving Mediterranean cuisine. Specialising in traditional rice dishes.

La Jaima de Marrakech €€ *Avenida Condimina 66; tel: (96) 515 28 16*. Moroccan cuisine. You can find a great deal here with the lamb couscous dinner that includes beverage and dessert for a reasonable €18. Closed Tuesday.

Jumillano €€€+ *Cesar Elguezabal, 62-64; tel: (96) 521 29 64*. Traditional Alicantine cuisine. Bull's tail stew is the speciality of the house. Closed Sunday in summer.

Romero € *Avenida Costa Blanca 130; tel: (96) 521 1215*. One of the few Spanish restaurants to actually include innovative veggie dishes along with *paella* and *pinchitos* (kebabs).

Yale €€ *Teniente Alvarez Soto 6; tel: (96) 520 43 44*. You'll find home-style cooking and *tapas* at reasonable prices; friendly atmosphere. Closed Sunday.

ALMORADI

El Cruce €€ *Camino de Catral 156; tel: (96) 570 03 56*. Good find for vegetarians – the vegetables come straight from the farm. Closed Sunday and Monday evenings.

ALTEA
El Canonge € *Calle Mayor 1; tel: (95) 584 4305*. A friendly small restaurant specialising in traditional local fare.

Recommended Restaurants

CALPE

La Fosa €€ *Ifach 3; tel: (96) 583 53 24.* An inexpensive restaurant specialising in *paella* and *fondue*. International cuisine also offered. Closed Monday in winter.

La Muralla € *Avenida de Diputacion 31; tel: (96) 583 2333.* An inexpensive Chinese restaurant with plenty of choice.

Playa € *Esplanada del Puerto; tel: (96) 583 00 32.* Excellent grilled fish and seafood dishes. Closed February.

Tango €€€ *Playa del Pope; tel: (96) 579 22 84.* Regional cuisine, specialising in *paella*. Relaxed, rustic atmosphere.

CARTAGENA

La Tartana €–€€ *Puerta de Murcia 14; tel: (96) 850 0011.* Lunch, supper and *tapas,* next to the old town. Regional, modern food.

DÉNIA

Club Nautico € *Suertes del Mar; tel: (96) 578 1083.* Inexpensive traditional cuisine featuring a wide variety of rice dishes. Closed Monday.

El Asador del Puerto €€€+ *Plaza del Raset 10-11; tel: (96) 642 3482.* Superb restaurant specialising in wood-oven roasted meats. Elegant surroundings.

El Raset €€€ *Bellaviata 7; tel: (96) 578 5040.* A pleasantly swish restaurant which attracts a loyal local clientele. Excellent for seafood.

El Comercio €€ *Marques del Campo 17; tel: (96) 578 5691.* International cuisine, featuring several different kinds of pizzas.

Romano €€€+ *Avenida del Cid 3; tel: (96) 642 1789.* An

upmarket, elegant restaurant serving Spanish and international cuisine. Good wine list. Closed Monday.

ELCHE

Els Capellans €€€+ *Porta de la Morera 14; tel: (96) 545 8040/661 0011.* Traditional rice dishes with a Mediterranean flavour. Excellent service and presentation.

La Finca €€€+ *Partida de Perleta 1-7; tel: (96) 545 6007.* You may consider this restaurant to be a bit pricey, but it is well worth the expense. Fresh produce is used in all its Mediterranean-style dishes. Closed Sunday evening and Monday.

El Granaino €€€ *Jose Maria Buch 40; tel: (96) 546 0147.* Excellent classy restaurant serving traditional Spanish cuisine. Closed two weeks in August.

La Magrana €€€ *Carretera Elche-Alicante, 2-3km; tel: (96) 545 8216.* Delightful restaurant where you can choose from more than 36 different varieties of *paella* and rice dishes.

GUARDAMAR DEL SEGURA

Rincon de Pedro €€ *Nicaragua 2, Cibeles 2; tel: (96) 572 8095.* Typical restaurant specialising in traditional rice and seafood dishes. Closed Wednesday.

JAVEA

121 € *Partida Montgo 121; tel: (96) 579 1237.* British-run restaurant serving international cuisine. Good for families.

Tasca Tonis € *Carrer Major 2; tel: (96) 646 1851.* A cheap and cheerful restaurant, popular with locals. Good *tapas* at the bar.

MURCIA

Alegría de la Huerta €-€€ *Plaza de San Juan 1; tel: (96) 821 7481.* Popular regional dishes and *tapas*.